BEGINNING
GO

BEGINNING
GO

Peter Shotwell and Susan Long

TUTTLE PUBLISHING
Tokyo • Rutland, Vermont • Singapore

Published by Tuttle Publishing, an imprint of Periplus Editions (HK) Ltd., with editorial offices at 364 Innovation Drive, North Clarendon, Vermont 05759 U.S.A.

Library of Congress Cataloging-in-Publication Data
Shotwell, Peter, 1941-
Beginning go / by Peter Shotwell and Susan Long.
    p. cm.
ISBN-10: 4-8053-0955-5
ISBN-13: 978-4-8053-0955-1
1. Go (Game) I. Long, Susan, 1946- II. Title.
GV1459.5.S55 2008
794'.4—dc22
                    2007022915

Distributed by

North America, Latin America & Europe
Tuttle Publishing
364 Innovation Drive, North Clarendon, VT 05759-9436 U.S.A.
Tel: 1 (802) 773-8930; Fax: 1 (802) 773-6993
info@tuttlepublishing.com
www.tuttlepublishing.com

Japan
Tuttle Publishing
Yaekari Building, 3rd Floor, 5-4-12 Osaki, Shinagawa-ku,Tokyo 141 0032
Tel: (81) 3 5437-0171; Fax: (81) 3 5437-0755
tuttle-sales@gol.com

Asia Pacific
Berkeley Books Pte. Ltd.
61 Tai Seng Avenue, #02-12, Singapore 534167
Tel: (65) 6280-1330; Fax: (65) 6280-6290
inquiries@periplus.com.sg
www.periplus.com

First edition
11 10 09 08   6 5 4 3 2 1

Printed in Canada

TUTTLE PUBLISHING® is a registered trademark of Tuttle Publishing, a division of Periplus Editions (HK) Ltd.

Table of Contents

Acknowledgments

We would like to thank all the people who made this book possible: Ed Walters, William Notte, and Kathy Wee of Tuttle Publishing; our agent Jim Fitzgerald; the past and present hard workers of the American Go Association; the members of the Brooklyn Go Club, our "local" for so many years; the engaging students and faculty of New York City's Elizabeth Irwin High School; Anders Kierulf for his Smart Go diagram program; John Fairbairn for his contributions to Go history; and, especially, Richard Bozulich for his insights into the finer points of playing the game.

On the Go board there are 360 intersections plus one. The One is supreme and gives rise to the other numbers because it occupies the center and governs the four quarters. The number 360 corresponds to the number of days in the lunar year. The division of the Go board into four quarters symbolizes the four seasons. There are 72 intersections on the sides, like the number of five-day weeks in a year. The balance of Yin and Yang is the model for the equal division of the 360 stones into black and white that come into play like the passage of day and night.

Based on *The Classic of Go*
by Chang Ni c. 1050 AD

Introduction

A number of years ago, Peter and I were giving a Go workshop to a group of my high school students as part of a three-day study of Japan. As I looked around the room, there were 20 students in deep concentration over their boards. I was surprised and curious by their level of interest and involvement. I asked several players what they liked about the game and one young man came up with an answer that the others agreed said it all: "It makes you think."

Games have been played throughout time by children and adults and seem to have been a part of every culture. Archeological records tell us that people have played games for thousands of years, so there must be something in the human brain that is attracted to challenges, new experiences, and being involved in creative competition.

There are physical games which challenge skill, strength, and strategy; there are games of chance where winning is often a function of luck; there are word games; there are board and computer games with a story element attached to them. And then there are strategic games where thinking, learning, and focus are essential parts of truly understanding their infinite variations.

I have asked friends and colleagues the question "Why do you think people play games?" Answers have ranged from "They're fun, relaxing, challenging, interactive, social; they focus your intelligence and reduce stress." I'm sure you have and will have many reasons of your own to add to the list.

Go is a game of patterns, territory, strategies, and focus. It is equally appealing to adults, teenagers, and children. With its special handicapping feature, a reasonable game can be played between beginners, novices, and experienced players. I have watched the enjoyment of strong Go players as they introduce the game to children and pass the mysteries of this unique activity to another generation.

I also remember working with a sixth grader on her writing skills, and before each session, I would spend fifteen minutes teaching her Go. This was time well spent because she was then able to move right into our writing work after the calming effect that Go seemed to have on her. By the way, at the end of the school year, she was a far better player than me, and her parents bought her a Go set of her own.

We live in a world where we are bombarded with distractions, noise, and visual images that often make it difficult to think about just one thing at a time. The young girl I mentioned hit upon one of the wonders of bringing your attention to focus tightly on a single process and idea. I believe there is a positive outcome that rewards the brain for that singular attention.

But enough philosophy and psychology! Go is our favorite game and I hope that this introduction and book will spark your interest. And most importantly, don't forget that Go is not only interesting, it's FUN!

What is Go?

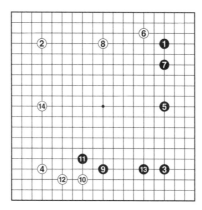

The beginning of a "peaceful" professional 19x19 Game

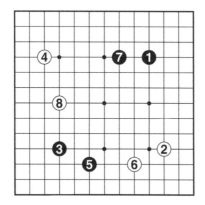   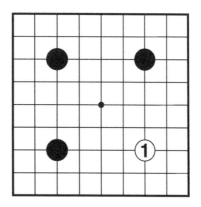

On the left, the beginning of a "less peaceful" amateur 13x13 game, showing off some typical corner enclosures. On the right on a 9x9 board, White is opening against a beginner who has been given three handicap stones by Igowin, a free, downloadable Internet program.

Go is . . . an ancient board game which takes simple elements—line and circle, black and white, stone and wood—combines them with simple rules and generates subtleties which have enthralled players for millennia. Beyond being merely a game, Go can take on other meanings to enthusiasts: an analogy with life, an intense meditation, a mirror of one's personality, an exercise in abstract reasoning, or, when played well, a beautiful art in which Black and White dance across the board in delicate balance. But most important for all who play, Go is challenging and fun.

—From the American Go Association Website
(www.usgo.org)

Go is a game of surrounding and capturing both stones and territory. In fact, the original name in Chinese is "the surrounding game." As will become clear in a few pages, you will find that as you try to surround, you may be getting surrounded yourself!

As shown above, and on the cover, Go is played with round, black and white pieces called *stones*. Western players like to use Japanese-style stones because they are lozenge-shaped and can be held between the index and second finger when putting them down on the board. The stones do not move after this, except, as you will see, when they are *captured*. (Go terms will be italicized the first time they appear—see the glossary for further details).

Probably, the surrounding idea was inspired by early Chinese methods of hunting big game animals. Being practical, they did not like to do anything dangerous unless they were sure to win. They surrounded their prey in great numbers, cast nets to immobilize them, and then sent in dogs, before closing in with their spears.

This is very different than the Western idea of directly attacking with full force, as chess pieces like to do. You will find that crafty kind of thinking is a highlight of Go playing, because it involves not only capturing "real" things like stones and groups of stones, but also "empty" spaces. But then, the cultivation of empty spaces might have encouraged thoughts about agriculture in the early days of Go. Or vice versa!

So, if you pursue Go history a little further, you will find that the surrounding idea is the basis of a Chinese "philosophy of action" that was formed about 500 to 300 BC. Ever since, it has been marveled at as the basis of Eastern thinking about Go, love, war, politics, business and life itself.

Next, you might also be tempted to read novels such as the brooding *Master of Go*, by Nobel Prize winner Yasunari Kawabata, or the disturbing *The Girl Who Played Go*, which takes place during the horrors of the Japanese occupation of Manchuria in WWII.

On a more peaceful side, in the East there is a two-thousand-year-old legacy of golden-tongued Go-playing poets who praised the game as one of the Four Arts of the gentleman and lady, along with calligraphy, painting and music.

In more modern days, there have been recent movies such as the cult hit, *Pi*, or the up-coming *Shibumi*, based on the 1970s international thriller by Trevanian, which has some of the most lyrical descriptions of the game ever written in English. For those serious about their Go, there is *The Go Masters*, the first Japanese-Chinese collaborative venture, and *The Go Master* about Go Seigen, perhaps the greatest player of all time.

Besides the literary efforts, there is a wonderful artistic element to Go. Eastern cultures have traditionally emphasized not only what their cultural objects do, but also what they look like. The result is that their top-quality Go sets have been unequalled in beauty.

In Japan, the best white stones have traditionally been cut from thick, softly grained clam shells harvested from only one beach, while the black stones still come from only a few special slate mines.

The best of the massive 8-inch-thick wooden Go boards that you see in Edo period *ukiyo-e* prints are cut to show off certain grain patterns from five-hunred-year-old *kaya* trees. Three other features of the boards are special cutout sections on the bottom to equalize the exposure and prevent cracking, elaborately carved legs, and slightly longer lengths over widths, so they look square to the players. The simple round forms of the bowls that hold the stones contrast with the squareness of the boards, especially when they are carved from rare hardwoods.

The Chinese have matched this almost-sacred regard for the game by making their stones and boards from precious minerals, jewels, pearls, and rhinoceros horns, while the Koreans have built boards with wires underneath so they made musical sounds when stones were played upon them.

If you want to know more about all this—where to find the poetry of Go or perhaps why Russell Crowe got so exasperated about the game in *A Beautiful Mind,* or how Japanese emperors sponsored deep-thinking theorists of the game for 400 years—these and other tidbits of Go's long history and influence are in my articles in the Bob High Memorial Library, on the American Go Association website.

These articles are quite long, however, so there is a condensed version in my first book, *Go! More Than a Game,* which also teaches from games played on ascending bigger boards.

My second book, *Go Basics,* uses a different approach. By using only professional 9x9 games, it focuses on the fundamental strategic concepts of Go without the distractions caused by the sometimes daunting size of the larger boards.

Beginning Go, on the other hand, has some brand-new teaching techniques and is meant for absolute beginners who want to start playing immediately and want a quick introduction.

About Beginning Go

We hope you will find out what Go can do for you by reading *Beginning Go*, because it has a number of teaching features that appear for the first time in a Western book.

It begins by using a simple method to solve the biggest difficulties that newcomers face—deciding when a game has ended, which groups of stones are *alive* and which are *dead*, and what the score is.

As any Go teacher or Internet Go chat group will tell you, frustrated beginners often waste a lot of time and many give up on the game before these rather simple ideas become clear.

Another unique feature of *Beginning Go* is that it uses 9x9 beginners' games to show mistakes of players like you. Most books use only high-level professional ones to teach you what you should do. We do that, but we also try to emphasize what you shouldn't do, because we feel you will more easily be able to avoid falling into bad habits that will effect your development as a player.

There is also a unique approach for teaching opening moves to handicap Go.

Lastly, with the Internet expansion of the last few years, there is an ocean of Go information that has appeared. However, it is generally not well organized and *Beginning Go* was written as a guide to that disorder.

For instance, there are thousands of problems available to be solved on sites like www.goproblems.com, so there is no need to include a lot of them in this book. However, there are no explanations of the basic principles, so we have included a few key problems at the end of most of the chapters that relate to the points discussed. These will launch you into problem-solving with a basic understanding that will make this interesting activity a much more enjoyable experience.

In sum, it is hoped that you will find how really great the ancient game of Go is, and why, for as many as 4,000 years, millions of people in the East and hundreds of thousands in the West have already done so!

CHAPTER ONE

The Art of Capturing

Let's explain the art of capturing stones first. Then, in the next few chapters, you see how capturing stones leads to the idea of surrounding the most empty spaces and why the basic principles of Go are not very complicated.

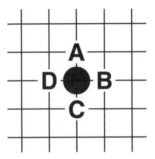

In the West, we say that a Black stone like the one above has four liberties (*A*, *B*, *C* and *D*).

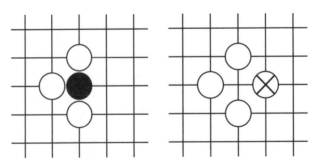

Taking turns, players put stones down one at a time on the intersections, so these teaching diagrams assume that Black is making other moves on the board.

These stones do not move afterwards, except when their liberties have been lost by being *sur-rounded* with stones of the other player. Then they are removed from the board.

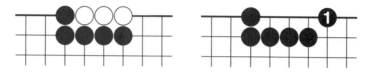

In one sense, having liberties means that other stones can *attach* there to form *groups*, as these diagrams indicate. The stone has the "freedom to grow," and you can imagine groups of stones as having arms and legs that are holding them together.

In this case, however, the stones of the White group has been surrounded on the side and removed after B1 *takes*. Like fallen warriors, they will not return to the fray.

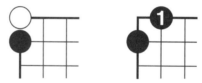

This lonely white stone in the corner has only one liberty and B1 takes that away.

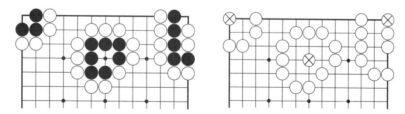

Larger groups that have an internal space (called an *eye*) can also be captured.

At the end of the *X*-marked capturing moves, the White stone has gained liberties, while the Black stones have lost theirs.

This is sometimes confusing to beginners because the capturing White stone seems to be surrounded first, but the end result of a play is what is important. Go is like a polite conversation—I say something and then you respond and then I answer and you respond. Go is a game of "back and forth" that you will soon get used to, but unlike the mutual destruction of chess, it is a game of evolution and growth.

Playing the Capture Game

With these thoughts in mind, play a few *capture games* with a friend or at a local Go club. You can even find people on the Internet servers to play with you.

If you don't have a Go set, begin on a 9x9 board such as the one included in this book that you can copy and enlarge. Play with pennies and dimes, or beans of two different colors. Small poker chips will also do if you enlarge the board.

It is strongly suggested that you stick to the 9x9 boards until you are more familiar with the surrounding concepts of the game. The principles of Go are the same for all sizes of boards and you will learn much more quickly because you can focus on the learning points more easily.

Begin with an empty board, play alternately, and try to be the first to capture a stone. If your companion is more experienced, put down a few stones for yourself as a handicap. It's not real Go, but you will find it is fun.

However, some odd, inexplicable situations will turn up, **so stop and don't play anymore!** Read why you should do this in the next chapter, and you will discover that surrounding and *killing* stones is only a small part of this great game. You will see why the capture of territory and the concept of *living* is much more important. Knowing this before playing too many capture games will create good habits of thought that will not have to be unlearned later.

Exercises

The Exercise sections will focus on major topics that were discussed in their chapters and point the way to the future. For further practice, go to the last chapter to find and get many graded sets of problems in books and on the Internet.

It is strongly recommended that you not only lay out the stones in the diagrams, but experiment with variations! Your game will improve much more rapidly.

The other major idea is to read and play both games and problems, read and play, read and play, and do not be afraid to try out new things.

And please don't play too slowly because you are agonizing over every move. If computers and top players cannot see everything that is going to happen, why do you think you will? Sometimes they have to go by intuition too.

As for experimenting, you may lose a few games, but your overall progress will be much faster. Good luck!

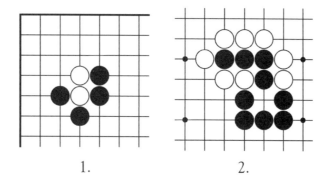

1.   2.

1. Black to play.

2. White to play.

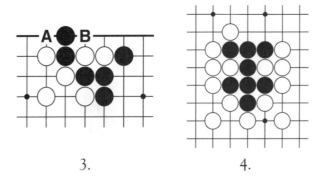

3.   4.

3. To take the two Black stones, should White play at A or B?

4. White to play.

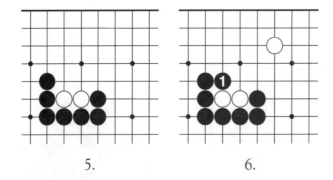

5.   6.

5. Black to play.

6. White to play and note the location of the stone in the upper-right.

Graduation Exercise

Graduation exercises take the concepts of the chapters an amusing step further and will require more thought than the preceding problems.

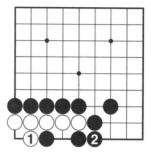

Things look pretty desperate for White, but there is one move still left to play. What is it? The answer will introduce you to the ideas in the next two chapters.

Answers

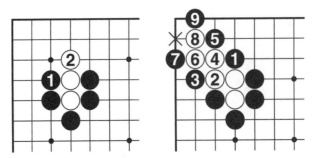

1. There is a good way and a bad way. The bad way is on the left—White can *run away* and cause trouble.

The good way on the right is called a *ladder* because it is like "helping" someone down some steps. X marks the spot where Black can *take* on the next move. Try to go back to the problem and see if you can visualize this sequence the way experienced players do.

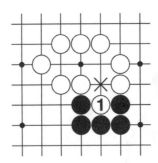

2. **Note after taking how W1 is in *atari* ("ah-tar-ee")—surrounded on all but one side.** Black can take back at X on the next move.

Saying "atari" is similar to saying "check" in chess. It need not be announced, although it is polite to do so until one is more experienced.

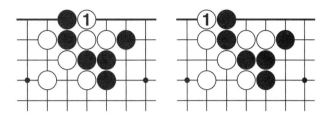

3. The wrong way: W1 in the left diagram puts White into self-atari and Black can take.

The right way: W1 on the right puts Black in atari and this enables White to take on the next move, no matter what Black does.

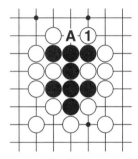

4. Black is dead after W1 ataries. Even if Black tries to run at *A*, the group is still in atari.

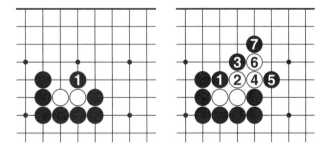

5. The White group is *virtually captured* after B1. If it tries to escape, it is still in atari.

Even if Black makes an inelegant mistake in *direction*, White will still die in a ladder.

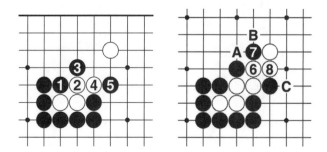

6. Here, if Black mistakenly tries the ladder method, White's stone is called a *ladder breaker*. White is alive because Black can atari at A, B, or C and escape. Beware of ladder breakers!

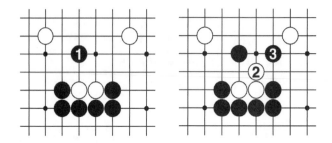

In this situation, Black must use a *net*, or a series of nets—handy tools to remember!

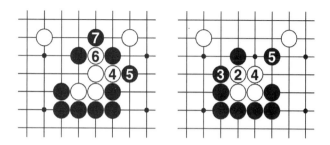

Voilà!

Graduation Exercise

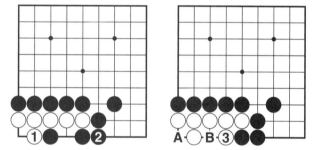

After W1, if Black does nothing or plays at B2, hoping to connect underneath, White will take and Black cannot play at either A or B.

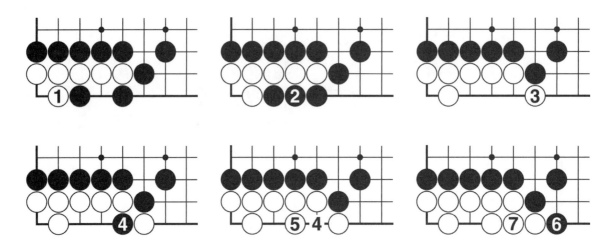

If B2, Black still cannot play at the former *A* or *B*. Find out what this peculiar situation means by browsing quickly through the next two chapters.

CHAPTER TWO

The Art of Living

A Quick Look at a Game

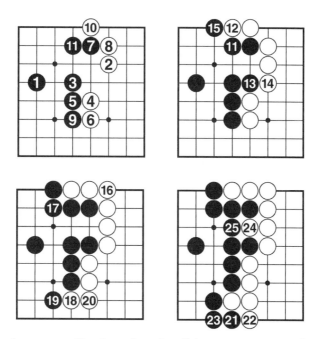

This game is illustrated on a smaller board and will be gone over in detail a little later in the book. For the time being, just notice how the patterns form because this chapter and the next will teach their meaning and how to make sense of what Go players are trying to do. You will learn why capturing is just part of the game.

This looks like a very simple game on what looks like the simplest of boards. Actually, it is adapted from one that was played by two professional go masters in a Japanese, quick-move TV tournament. At the end, when there are no empty spaces between the groups, you can see that the players have divided up the board rather evenly. Both realized that any Black stones played on the right, or any White stones played on the left, could easily be captured and taken off the board.

What this means is that you can surround not only stones, but also empty intersections.

In this game, many stones were threatened but none were surrounded and captured, so, if you count the *territories*, you would find that White controls 20 empty spaces and so has 20 points, while Black has 19.

But Black always moves first, (except in handicap games, which will be discussed later). This is an advantage, so 6^1/$_2$ points are customarily deducted from Black's score, and White "wins" by 7^1/$_2$ points.

"Wins" is in quotation marks because, given the value of the first move, winning in Go is always relative.

The half-points mean that there are no draws, as happens so frequently in chess.

Doesn't Go look easy and logical? But remember that these pros probably figured out the final results after their first few moves. In other words, on the 9x9 board, the biggest problem for experienced players is where to play in the *opening*.

However, what's confusing for beginners is not the beginning, which is where almost all go books start.

As you have already seen in this book and in your capture games, in the beginning you can put your stones down anywhere and try various lines of play.

However, in the ending, you can't, so deciding when the game is over and how to score it becomes the NUMBER ONE PROBLEM for beginners. It is by far the most common reason that some players abandon the game before its treasures are revealed!

So, unlike other Go books, we deal with counting the score first in this book. In doing so, the basic underpinnings of the game will be revealed in a natural way.

What follows will look like a more complicated game than the last one because Black makes two groups. Actually it isn't, because the players were only mid-level amateurs.

Please just glance at the overall patterns as the game develops. Its real purpose is to show how a seemingly complex result is so easily countable, and why many say that Go is the most interesting of all board games. The reasons why the players played one way or another will be discussed later, when they will be more understandable.

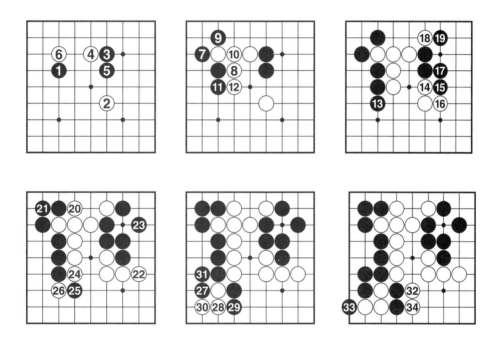

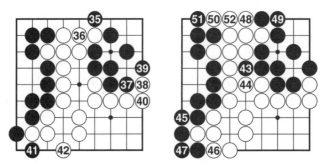

After B41 puts White's three marked stones into atari, White must take with W42.

Since the players are convinced that any stones they might play inside the other's area will *die*, each *passes* their turn to play.

Again, if either disputes this and thinks they can play on to make more points, they are welcome to try. The other player must then decide if there is any threat of that stone *living* or attacking vulnerable points and must either pass or play.

If the opponent's stone is answered, it will not affect the score. However, if there is no answer and the play proves fruitless, it will reduce the teritory by one point per stone.

It is strongly advised in the beginning to answer these kinds of moves until the dynamics of the game become clear.

So, who won? The next chapter will show you how easy it is to count this game.

CHAPTER THREE

Who Has Played the Most Living Stones?

Counting

Forget for a moment everything you might have heard about how Go games are scored—territory, keeping captured stones, not keeping captured stones, Chinese rules, Japanese rules, etc. and etc.

Think for a moment of Go as a game whose winner has been able to put down the most living stones on the board.

So what happens if these players keep putting down stones to increase their score? In the West, this has been called the "Stone Counting" method and it is somewhat based on the traditional Chinese way of counting. This is the first time it has been used in an English language Go book not only to count, but to uncover the underlying principles of Go.

First, you will see how it makes a complicated result on the board very easy to score.

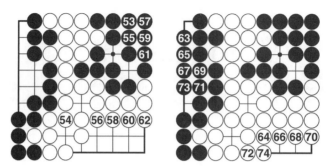

The players keep putting down stones but Black must stop when there are only two empty spaces in each group. Why?

Because if Black *filled in* one of the empty spaces in either group, that group would have only one liberty and White could capture Black's stones on the next move.

In other words, the black groups each have two *eyes*, or what the Chinese call *breaths* and the Koreans call *houses*. As you can see, in Go you need two of them to make a group and anything attached to them alive—they can never be killed.

But as for counting and finding who was the better player, after they have made an equal number of moves (since Black played first), White can put down three more stones on the board before being left with two eyes. So White played more efficiently in surrounding stones and territory.

We hope you can now see how Go becomes a game of efficiency and cleverness instead of an exercise in simply killing the most stones.

Because the Black player was a little weaker than the one who played White, before they started they had agreed on a 3½ point handicap for Black instead of the usual 6½. So White wins by 6½ points.

Again, we want to remind you that if your opponent plays a stone or stones to try to live inside your groups and you answer with an equal amount of stones, it will not affect the score. However, if you think it is a foolish move and don't answer, it will cost that player one point per stone.

Still, if there is any doubt, it is strongly advised you answer these kinds of moves until the dynamics of the game become clearer. If you don't, get ready for many surprises!

Varieties of Two-eyed Groups

You will find that the shapes of two eyes inside of the living groups that are attached to them can come in many sizes and forms.

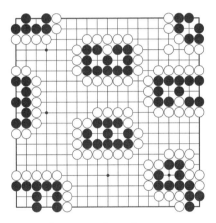

White can never take these two-eyed groups by placing a stone in one of their eyes because they will always have one liberty left. The attacking stone can be taken on the next "move."

In this case, "move" is in quotation marks because it wouldn't really be a move, since no stone would need to be placed down for the capture. Thus, in the Japanese and Chinese systems of counting, suicides are not permitted because they are non-moves.

The Japanese and Chinese Methods of Counting

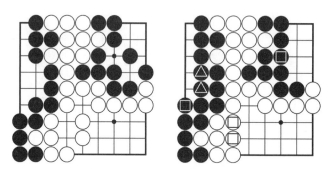

In the Stone Counting system, the two stones that White captured at the bottom would not be counted because they are not on the board. In other words, Black has lost two points in terms of stones, plus the two points of territory that they occupied so that White can put down two more stones when counting. This makes the capture of two stones worth four points.

The Japanese system used by Western players is different because it counts both the stones and empty territory that each player has gained. Thus, Japanese-style Go bowls have lids that are up-ended to hold the *prisoners* that each player has captured.

At the end of this game, White's two prisoners would be put back into Black's territory as indicated by the triangle-marked stones. In addition to the two empty spaces that White has gained, this reduces Black's score by two for the same total of four points.

Being aesthetically minded, and for ease of counting, the Japanese like to arrange the stones in units of five, if possible. The square-marked stones have been moved to make this arrangement.

It is easy to see that White has 16 points and Black has 13, so again, White wins by 6½ points with the handicap counted in.

You may encounter the Chinese method of counting at some point and it is illustrated in the last exercise of this chapter where the three systems are compared. They count stones and territory of only one side, don't keep prisoners, and, at the end, compare the total with half the number of intersections of an empty board.

However, neither the Japanese nor the Chinese ways of counting make the inner dynamics of Go stand out like the Stone Counting system, so it is advised that you use it to discover the peculiarities of groups that are alive and groups that are dead.

Life and Death

In determining the life or death of a group, there are some sub-categories of the concept of two eyes that are important to learn.

For example, not everything that looks like an eye is necessarily one—some eyes are *false* **and others are vulnerable.**

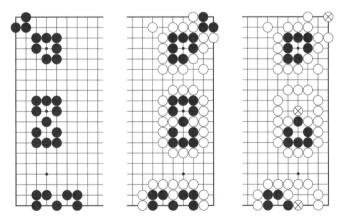

To give you practice at how there is no real up-and-down or right-and-left in Go, see how groups look when they are reversed. Try to follow the killing of these three groups from left to right as if they occupied the same position on a board.

The lesson the top group demonstrates is that stones linked diagonally are not connected if they can be cut. When White surrounds that group, it ends up being divided into two independent one-eyed, dead groups.

Each of the two groups below it have two false eyes, both of which can be taken.

In situations like these, the players will know they are dead. Unless they are becoming surrounded themselves, they will not make unnecessary capturing moves.

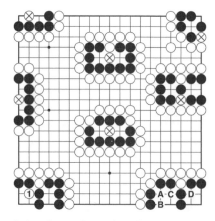

The difference between life and death in these kinds of shapes is sometimes just a single stone on the right or wrong intersection.

Inside these groups, White has played on the vital spots and now they have only one eye.

If Black could have gotten there first, they would have been alive.

In the middle-right group, the *X*-marked White stone has taken the vital point that would have meant life for Black—Black is in atari.

In the lower-right, Black is dead because any White move at *A-D* cannot be dealt with. White *A* would be *double atari*. If White plays *B* and Black *responds* with *A*, White *C* would decide the issue. White *D* is like W1 in the lower-left corner.

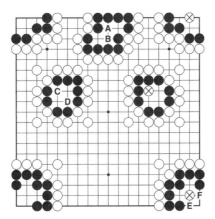

Other shapes are vulnerable, too.

The upper corners illustrate a five-space group. See how it is alive if Black gets to play a stone at the vital point, and how it is dead if White gets to go there first.

The middle group at the top is safe—if White *A*, then Black *B* and vice versa. However, if Black can get stones down at *E* and *F*, the group would have two eyes and live.

However, if White can play both *A* and *B*, the group is dead.

With the group in the center-left, a White play at *C* or *D* will *kill* the group and it can only be saved if Black can put down stones on both points. The center-right group illustrates this.

In the lower-left and lower-right, try to visualize how, if White plays the *X*-marked stone and Black tries *E*, then White *F* prevents two eyes from forming—and vice-versa.

You will soon begin to automatically recognize these shapes and apply the proverb that advises, "Often the best place to play is where your opponent would like to."

Dead Big Eyes

Let's round off this chapter by returning to where it began.

You will see how one has to be careful when completing the Stone Counting process!

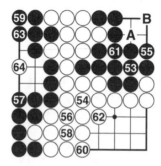

For example, here Black has managed to lose both groups by not thinking about where stones should be put down—the group on the right side ends with the four-space dead shape that appeared in the left-middle portion of the previous diagram. If Black plays at A, White plays at B or vice versa.

On the left, Black has a classic five-space dead group and W64 plays on the vital spot. If Black had played there first, there would have been two eyes. These are called dead *big eyes*.

White has made a big eye too, but it is large enough to make two eyes if there is a threat. In this case, Black doesn't have enough liberties to make trouble.

Conclusion

Congratulations! Now you know enough to start playing real Go!

Exercises

Now that you know what life and death are all about and why this knowledge is a key to good Go playing, we will tease your wits a little.

We have seen how ladders can lead to the execution of groups and in the next chapter, we will look at how groups of stones can remain alive. In the meantime, let's look at how *sacrifices* are used. You will soon see how, when played skillfully, they can become an art form.

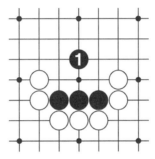

1. This is one of the most famous patterns in Go—we see how Black is trying to *escape*. Hint: It will take a sacrifice below B1 to do it!

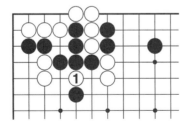 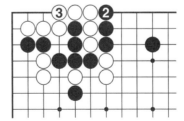

2. So let's take this one step further and really tease your brain! White has made a similar approach that was tried in Exercise 1. Will it work? B2 certainly doesn't!

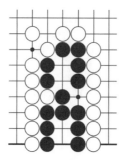

3. If it is Black's turn, one move will save this group, but what if it is White's move?

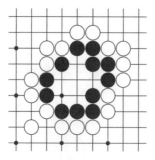

4. Alive or dead?

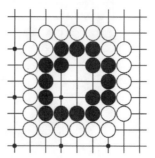

5. The inside shape is the same. Pretend that White is in danger of being surrounded. How many stones would it take to actually remove Black from the board?

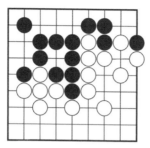

6. This game between two beginners is not finished and it is White's turn to play. Try to find the best final moves and then score it using the Japanese method. White has taken two prisoners up to this point. It would be best to lay this out on a board.

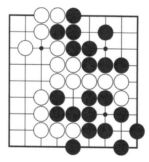

7. Similarly, finish this game off and count it with the Stone Counting system. Black has captured two stones and it is White's turn to play.

Graduation Exercise

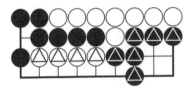

The two marked groups are in a *capturing race*. Assume the upper groups are attached to safe groups and it is White's turn. Try laying this out on a board to see who will win and why.

Answers

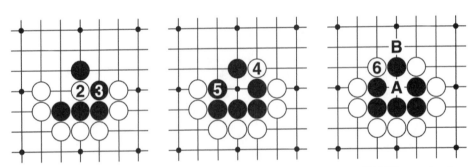

1. Easy as pie! This clever combination is called the *crane's nest*. If White A, then Black B and vice versa.

   Take a look at the right-center group on page 36 and see how similar it is to this situation.

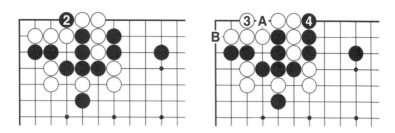

2. The sacrifice of B2 lays the trap.

Next, White is in atari. If White A, then Black B finishes the sequence since White has only one liberty and can't escape. Black has three liberties.

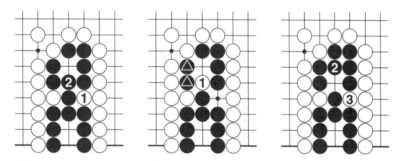

3. Alive!...Dead! W1 ataris the marked stones and Black is left helpless after B2 with one eye and one false eye. We saw this pattern before and you will see it many more times in your games!

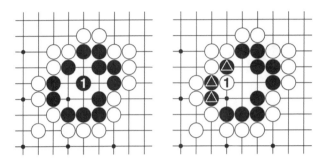

4. In this six-point group—sometimes called a *rabbity-six* because it seems to have a head and long ears—if Black gets to play B1, Black is alive.

Therefore, White can play there or at W1 where it would be double atari on the marked stones which would automatically kill the group.

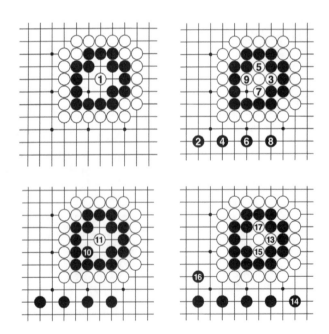

5. After W1, the process begins and sometimes doesn't seem to end! meanwhile, Black is

moving elsewhere on the board.

W11 must be played on the vital spot.

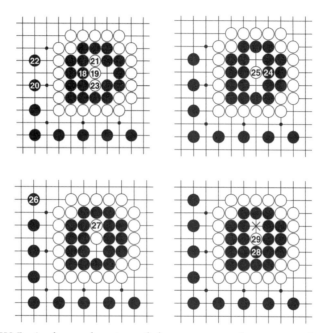

So must W19 and W25. At least the size of the groups to be captured is decreasing!

Finally White reaches the point where Black is in atari and cannot play at X because of self-atari. But Black still gets the next move somewhere else. There have certainly been a lot of unanswered Black moves! See if you can figure out the formula for how much it takes to capture these types of empty spaces.

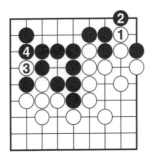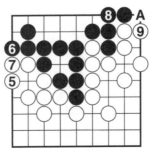

6. Can Black play at A next?

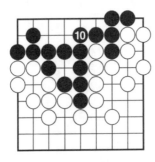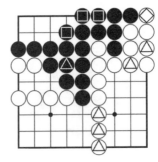

No! It would be self-atari and White could take. Therefore Black must first play B10 as in the diagram on the left.

The resulting space in the upper-right corner is called a neutral or *dame* ("dah-may") point, which can be filled by either player with no resulting gain or loss. Usually players fill them in with alternate turns, so in this case, White puts a stone down there that is marked with a diamond.

If the Stone Counting method is being followed, make sure that the players each put down an equal amount of stones—meaning White must play the last stone. If all the dame are filled and White has nowhere to play, subtract a point from Black or add one to White. With the Japanese method of counting empty spaces and not stones, this is usually not important.

The square-marked stones are Black prisoners. The triangle-marked stones have been moved to make counting easier.

It is easy to see that White has 33 points and Black seven before the handicap for going first is factored in. If this handicap, called the *komi* ("koh-me") in Japanese, is 6½ points, White has won by 32½ points. Black should try taking two stones for the next game.

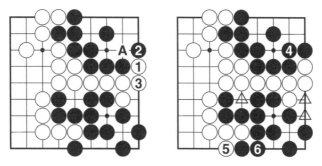

7. Notice in this short sequence how White is on the offensive and picks up points on the right side and then gets to play at the bottom because Black must defend at A. It would be big if White got to play there. The players then automatically fill in the marked spaces.

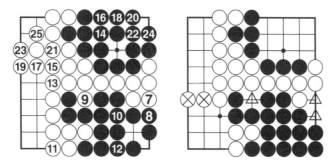

With the Stone Counting system on the left, after the neutral points are filled, the players continue to put down stones until Black is left with two two-eyed groups and the players have played an even number of moves. White has 13 and Black has four so White wins by nine points *on the board*.

The results for the Japanese System are on the right. The two *X*-marked prisoners are placed back on the board inside White's territory. All the empty intersections between the groups must be filled in, but be careful it doesn't affect the strategic situation. Therefore it is strongly suggested that you play these in order until you are very familiar with the process.

White has 19 and Black has 12 so White wins by seven points on the board.

Why is there a difference? Because Black has made two groups and so could not fill the extra two points of territory in the Stone Counting process.

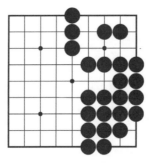

Just to be complete, this is the Chinese result, though they would arrange it further by remembering the amount of Black's territory, adding it to the number of Black stones and then comparing this to half the total number of intersections. The result is 81 divided by 2 equals 40½ minus 37 Black points equals 3½, the "equivalent" of a seven point White win in the Japanese system.

"Equivalent" is relative, though, since other factors are at work when counting with the Chinese system. Unlike the informal Stone Counting method, Black will gain a point by filling in the last dame point, and this doesn't "translate" to a half point in the Japanese system, since they don't count stones.

Another factor is that the Chinese stones-plus-territory counting does not "tax" Black for having made two groups when White has only made one, although this used to be the case.

Still another factor to consider is that Chinese Go is relatively "straightforward" in its approach to the rules—"What you see is what you get" well describes it—while the Japanese System has been a hodge-podge of ad hoc "rulings" for hundreds of years to account for some of the pecular shapes that Go stones can twist themselves into at the end of a game. This chapter has tried to give a taste of the different logic that proceeds from counting stones, territories or both, and why the Stone Counting method is best for beginners.

All this complexity has helped make Go a mathematician's paradise and it sometimes created crucial differences (and great arguments!) in international tournaments. So again, until you have a lot of Go playing under your belt, the best advice is to take "who wins" and by "how much" with big grains of salt!

Graduation Exercise

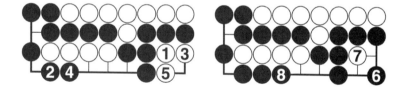

W5 puts Black into atari, but, as in problem 5, it will take some extra stones to actually capture, so so B8 puts White into atari. But there is a better way for White to play.

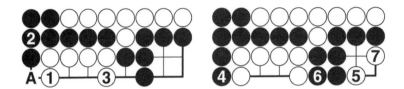

W1 is the clever move. Black must play B2 to get to A. Meanwhile, White calmly plays W3 to form a big eye.

On the right Black is dead.

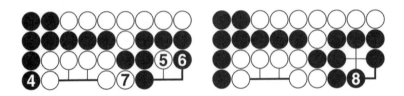

But if White makes a mistake, Black gets two eyes. And Black also has a clever move!

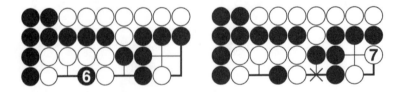

Because of self-atari, White can't take, and, after W7, neither side wants to play at the X-marked spot. We will have more to say about this in a future chapter, but in the meantime, try to work out some of the other possible ways to play this problem out.

CHAPTER FOUR
A "Simple" Game

The word "simple" has quotation marks around it because this is a professional game and no professional game is "simple." Not only are the players geniuses, but they have been working hard since early childhood and the strategies and techniques they study have developed over thousands of years.

So, in Go terms, this is more of a "peaceful" game than a simple one. We have already seen how it ended, but it was shown on an 8x8 board to demonstrate more vividly why no more moves could be made inside each player's groups. For teaching purposes, this is an adaptation of the full 9x9 version and it would be a good idea to lay out the stones on a board to follow the game. You will appreciate more of its subtleties!

The Opening Game

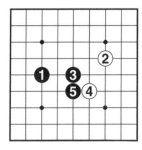

The players lay claim to each side of the board and Black aggressively takes the center point with B3. It is also a one-space jump, so there are no real weaknesses left behind by extending too far.

In 9x9 Go, control of the center can be important and in most professional 9x9 games, Black first takes the center point. It is suggested that you try this in your games, but remember that this is not so important on larger boards.

White makes a *forcing move* at W4. If B5 is not played, White will gladly occupy that intersection.

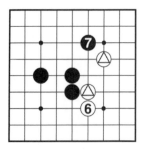 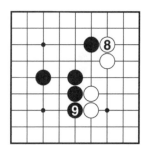

W6 is different, however, because it is not as big if White penetrates the lower side from the third line.

Black does not *answer* and instead makes the *knight's move* of B7, which is a much bigger threat because of the weakness of White's initial knight's move—it can be *cut* in two, so White must reinforce at W8. Then Black goes back to play the next biggest move on the board by defending the bottom with B9.

The Middle Game

The basic areas have been laid out, so the opening is over and the *middle game* begins. This is when *infighting* will start to take place as the players jostle for positions.

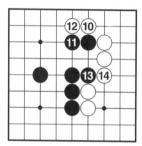

After the exchanges of W10-W14 have been made, it looks like Black has more territory than White. But remember that there is the 6½ point penalty for Black going first.

Notice how White *slid* along the upper edge with W10-12. There are more points to be made by doing this than at the bottom.

Also notice how Black does not answer W12, but pushes with B13, which threatens to *invade* White territory on the right.

And notice, also, how strong the formation is that Black makes with B11 and B13. This is called a *bamboo joint* and makes it impossible for White to push through.

The End Game

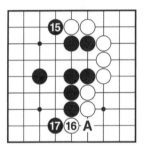

It is now the *end game* and, in your future Go games, you will play thousands of moves like these around the edges of the board.

Gradually, you will discover that some are more lucrative than others. Though the number of points at stake during any one move may not be many, mistakes in playing them in the right order can add up to large numbers!

After B15 blocks White's progress, White takes the opportunity to build more territory with W16, but then, after B17, A must be protected.

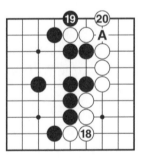

This gives Black the opportunity to play at the top with B19, which threatens an atari at A so White plays W20 to defend.

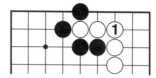

White could also play at W1, and this *solid connection* is usually better because it is not open. The reason for this will become clearer in the next chapter.

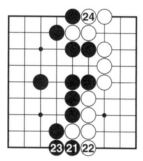 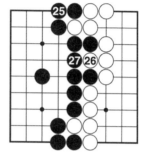

The players then fill in the final points and, with B27, the game ends, leaving White with 23 points and Black with 31. However, the 6½ point komi gives Black a 1½ point victory.

Exercises

As a reminder, again it is best to lay out the stones so the lessons will sink in and be more easily understood!

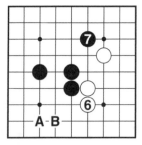

1. Let's look at the situation after the two knight's moves took place. What if White moved to A or B? What would be Black's simplest response?

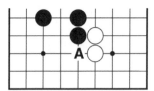

2. Whatever is going on at the top, Go players would certainly keep in mind the situation at the bottom. What are the other possible White moves if Black doesn't play at A (B9 in the game)?

Graduation Exercise

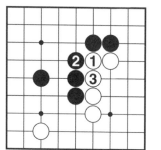 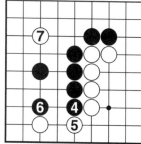

White has decided that resistance on the bottom is futile. Is there any hope of living at the top?

Answers

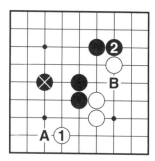

1. For amateurs, looking for a simple move with two meanings is the best advice. If White plays W1 or A, B2 takes a vast amount of territory and creates a severe weakness at B that White must defend. Because of the X-marked stone, a professional might make the game close, but it would be difficult to win. (On the other hand, Black won anyway.)

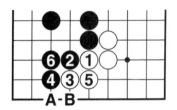 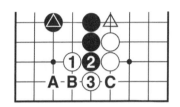 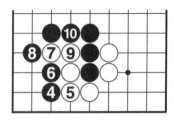

2. The same advice is good for amateurs when they are thinking about playing along the edges of the board. Until you gain some more experience, simplicity is best!

For example, W1 on the left is simple. After the response, later in the game when the value of the moves was less, A would be played by White or B would be played by Black. The value of moves like this will be discussed in Chapter Seven.

On the right is a more complicated maneuver. The possible responses depend on the surrounding circumstances. In this case, the stone and the absence of a protecting stone at the marked intersections are critical.

The most conservative follow-up for Black is possible because of the marked stone. The more adventurous choices of B and C in the middle diagram have the same results as the next set of possibilities.

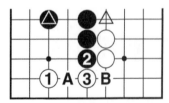 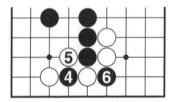 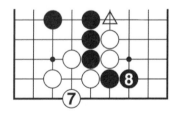

The big jump of W1 is also affected by the marked places. Black can play at A or B.

At this point things can get complicated and there is no one answer—the result will depend on the state of the rest of the board and the skill of the players.

For example, White will have the same problem on the right side that appeared in Exercise 5 of the first chapter. If Black moves at the marked intersection, White only has two liberties. There is also the question of whether the White group can stay alive on the left. If it does, to keep things even, Black must also live in the right corner. You would have to spend quite a bit of time trying to figure this out if you laid down the stones on a board. Imagine trying to play it out in your head in a game!

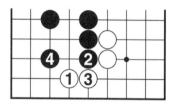 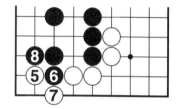

Another simple choice is W1. Black can only defend passively.

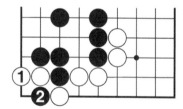 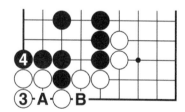

But White must not get greedy.

A nasty surprise waits at A or B. Black takes whether White fills or not. This is a pattern that one must always be alert about.

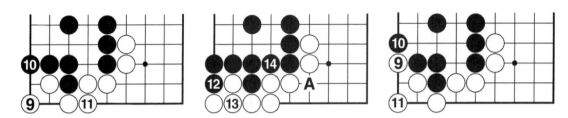

A safe way is still quite profitable for White, although A must still be played after B14.

A more dangerous way is on the right, but you might have to read the next chapter and do the exercises to understand the consequences. After that, come back and try to play it out on the full board.

Graduation Exercise

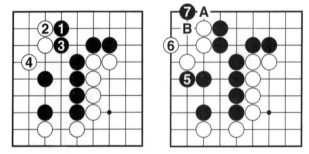

None whatsoever. If White B, Black A.

CHAPTER FIVE

Some Mysteries of Go: Seki, Ko, and the Second Rule of Go

Seki

This chapter will re-introduce *seki* ("seh-key") and introduce *ko* "(koh")", two of the more mysterious aspects of Go. They may have already occurred in your games and you may have solved the problem on your own, as many beginners do.

Seki is the easy one that occurs far fewer times than the more complicated concept of ko that follows.

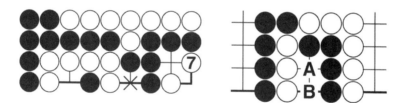

In these situations, if White tries to atari, it is self-atari and vice versa for Black, so neither will play in the disputed area. This is the essence of a seki and it occurs sometimes in games, either accidentally or deliberately as a strategy to save a group, depending on the skills of the players.

Under Japanese rules, none of the stones inside a seki are counted, even if there are uneven amounts. Nor are the empty spaces counted. In Chinese rules, the stones are counted but not the territory. The result, in either case, is like a bad marriage—two groups are locked in an unfriendly embrace that neither can escape.

There are many other ways to achieve (or avoid) seki which you will discover as you play your games—but for now it is sufficient to know that they exist and what to do (and what you can't do) about them. Here, for example, White would waste a move by playing at A under Japanese rules, but would gain a point under the Chinese and Stone Counting systems.

Ko

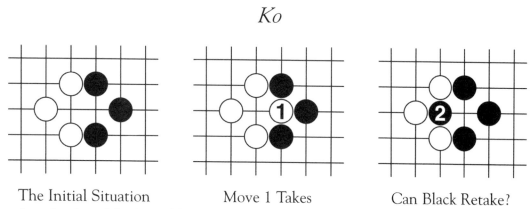

The Initial Situation   Move 1 Takes   Can Black Retake?

This taking back and forth could go on forever, hence the word ko in Japanese is derived from the Sanskrit word for "a long time."

The Second Rule of Go

The second rule of Go is that no situation can repeat itself. If there is a ko going on, a move must be made that changes the position on the board before the threatened stone can be retaken.

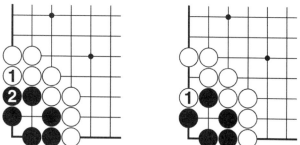

On the left, if White simply plays W1, B2 makes the smallest possible living group in Go.

But on the right, White tosses in W1 to set up a ko.

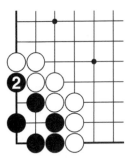 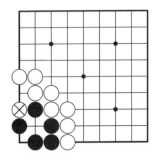

Since W1 did not take a stone, Black can immediately take back.

However, after B2, White cannot take back with the X-marked move because the board position would be the same as it was two moves before.

Therefore, White must find a move that threatens to make more points than the group involved in the ko is worth. This is called making a *ko threat*.

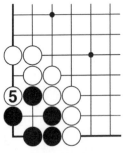 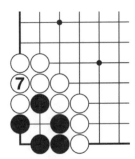

B4 Elsewhere   B6 Elsewhere

If Black answers the threat with B4 on another part of the board, White can come back and retake the ko with W5. Usually, there are many threats on the board so, as a ko progresses, the value of the threats will decrease until one or the other's threat is smaller than the value of the stones and territory involved in the ko. In this case, if what B6 threatens is smaller than the value of the Black group, W7 *fills* the ko.

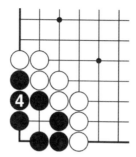

If White's first ko threat of W3 was not big enough, however, Black could fill the ko with B4 and live.

With these factors in mind, how do you calculate the value of a ko?

By winning the ko, in the Japanese system, Black saved five stones, the territory they were on, plus two points of empty intersections. That makes an initial total of 12 points, but it is only initial because the value of the threat that White made must be subtracted.

Suppose White's threat put five stones into atari, so when Black filled the ko and saved the group, White took them. That would have been a ten-point move (five stones and five points of territory) so the immediate value to Black for taking the ko was only two points, not 12.

There are other factions, as well, that often make a ko smaller than it might look at first. However, the overall strategic situation must also be factored in and looks can be deceiving!

Chapter Nine will give an example of a ko fight that went on for most of a game. It will show how the threats became smaller and smaller until winning the ko became irrelevant.

For now, however, as with seki, just be aware that strange things can happen on your Go board. Play them out and above all, don't be afraid to experiment!

Exercises

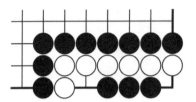

1. Is this a seki?

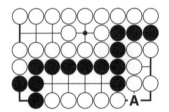

2. If White gets to play at A, Black would have only one eye and could be killed. But it is Black's turn. How can a seki save the situation for Black?

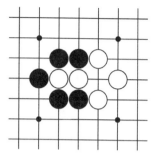

3. If Black takes on the next move, does White have to move elsewhere before retaking?

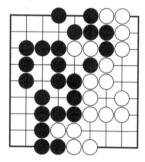

4. This amateur game is down to its final movements. What is about to happen in the upper-center? It is White's move. Is this related to ko?

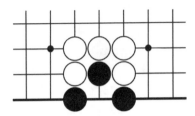

5. In this simplified position, should White start a ko?

Graduation Exercise

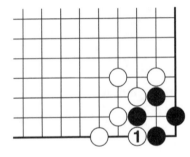

White has tried to start a ko with W1. In this kind of situation, would this always be a good idea? Try to work out all the considerations. There are quite a few and they won't be easy! For example, what if there is a second ko going on somewhere else on the board?

Answers

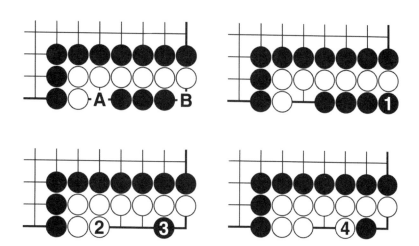

1. Yes. White cannot play at A or B without coming into self-atari. If Black tries anything, White will live.

Black also cannot move to the left, so neither will play unless a ko occurs with higher stakes.

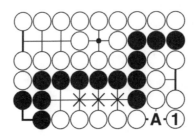

2. Once White takes with W1, whether A is filled or not, either side can fill up the X marked spaces until one empty one is left, thus producing the seki.

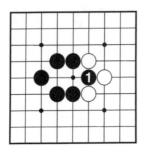 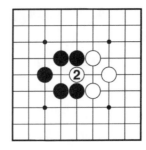

3. No. W2 makes a new position.

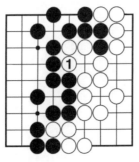 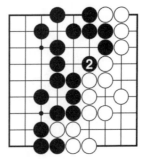

4. Ouch! This is called a *snap-back* because, well, it "snaps back." It has no relation to ko—B2 makes a new position.

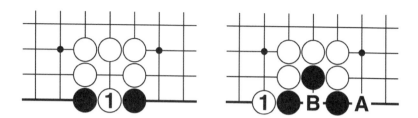

5. Starting a ko is a cumbersome way of dealing with this kind of situation. Instead, atari on the outside—Black cannot fill because it would be self-atari.

Black can only run away to A, so White would be able to take the two stones and make the beginning of two eyes.

Graduation Exercise

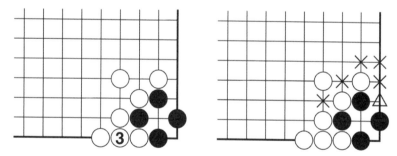

First of all, in its simplest form, White must make two moves to win it. Therefore, Black can get the benefit of two moves elsewhere. Plus, there are future ko threats at the X-marked spots which would enable some or even all of the Black group to survive. Note how few liberties the solid White group has and how Black is protected by the corner.

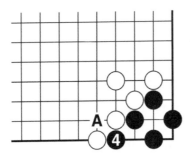 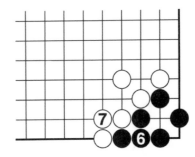

Again, in its simplest form, after B2 makes a bigger threat elsewhere and W3 responds, B4 takes back the ko. But now White has a problem—the value of the ko has increased enormously because Black is now threatening to expand along the side by playing at A.

As you can see, this could get very complicated, especially if there is another ko going on where the only rule that applies is that the same board position not be repeated. This is called the *super-ko* rule. In Japan, however, ko is only for consecutive moves, so the extremely rare *triple ko* causes a draw. Traditionally, this has been considered a bad omen because a 17th-century warlord was assassinated on the night one occurred in a game he was watching.

Offense and Defense: Sente and Gote

To conclude, in the last diagram, B6 is not a passive, defensive move, because White answers it. This makes B4 a move in *sente* ("sen-teh") and W7 a move in *gote* ("go-teh").

In a nutshell, sente is being on the offense, gote is being on the defense. As you can see, sente moves are worth more than gote moves—in this case, Black gets the benefit of having the next move while White earns nothing.

But these concepts will expand in scope, so keep their simple definitions in the back of your mind, until they are dealt with more fully after a look at a handicap game.

CHAPTER SIX

Handicaps, Ranks, and Styles of Play

Handicap Go

One of the glories of Go is its ancient handicap system—handicap points appear on the earliest surviving Go board. Without distorting any of the action or the skills needed, anyone can play interesting games with anyone else in the world.

Although the Chinese sometimes let the weaker player put handicap stones anywhere, traditionally the corner stones are put on the *star points*—the 4-4 points for 19x19 boards and the 3-3 points for the 9x9 size.

This location is somewhere between being a territorial move that lays claim to the corner and a move that radiates *influence* towards the center. In other words, it forces the weaker player to decide between taking present *profit* or waiting patiently for future gains. The same kind of thinking goes into the placement of handicap stones on the sides, if they are needed.

Handicap Go also encourages lots of thought about when to attack weak groups of the opponent in sente and get double-value for moves, and when to defend your own weak groups in gote and get less value, but more safety.

In other words, handicap Go makes you think very carefully about the balance and harmony of your game. And from this kind of thinking, you will learn more about Go's beauties!

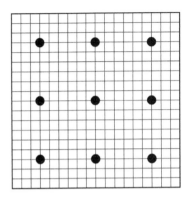 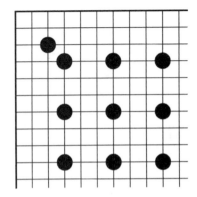

The traditional 9-stone handicap layout and arrangement for adding extra stones. Generally the corner 3-3 stones are put down before adding stones on the sides, although if that many are needed, it is suggested to play on smaller boards where the handicap stones are worth more.

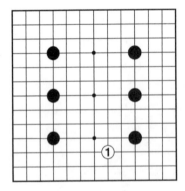 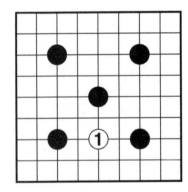

The beginning of a six- and a five-stone game on the 9x9 board.

In this chapter, we will follow a sample three-stone handicap game against *Igowin*, a popular on-line interactive program that is fun to play with to improve your game or keep it sharp. You can download it for free (at www.smart-games.com/igowin.html) to keep on your computer and games take only a few minutes.

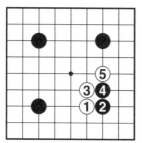 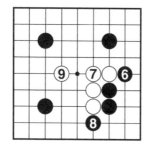

Black starts by comfortably staking out territory in the corner, while Igowin, who is White, builds an outside wall. But Igowin does not use the power of the wall very well and only jumps out one space with W9. Two spaces would not only have been safe, but it would have neatly split the two Black handicap stones on the left. Eventually, this error will cost White the game.

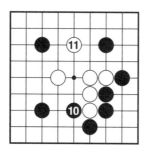 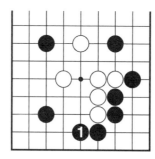 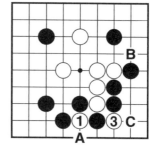

Uh oh! B10 returns White's mistake and W11 is one of the spots where Black should have played. Black is safe in the corner and doesn't need this overly cautious move which isn't even the best to connect.

B1 would be much better because it invites less trouble later on. For example, if W3 was played, White B becomes a threat because of the possibility of White C.

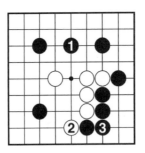 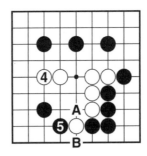

However, the corner group is *open* at both ends and could run away if trouble loomed. Even if it couldn't, the shape is good for making two eyes. If Black played B1 instead of B11 in the game and White attacked the lower-left corner stone with W4, Black could make a *clamp move* to connect—if White A, then Black B or vice versa.

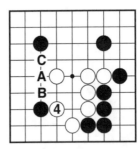 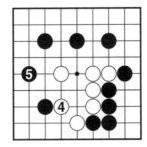

If White plays like this, to respond at A is too close—it invites trouble at B and C.

The play on the right is better—it would protect territory and confine White to the small area in the center. The best move combines offense and defense and now White could be attacked on all four sides, while Black would have the edges to extend from!

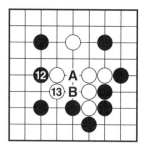

In any case, B12 is in the right area and puts some pressure on White, who does not have *eye-shape* yet.

In addition, B12 threatens a Black move at W13, which would end the game in Black's favor since White could only hope for territory in a small part of the top. So White moves there first, putting pressure on Black to defend the corner.

W13 also forms a bamboo joint, which is unbreakable and therefore a much sought-after connection. If Black ever plays B to try to cut White, White can play A and vice versa.

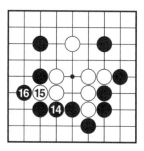
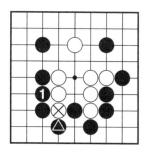

With B14, Black panics in trying to protect what doesn't have to be protected. On the other hand, maybe Black became simply greedy, thinking only of the territory B14 seemed to acquire. W15-B16 leaves Black in an awkward position.

Instead, see how B1 would have sealed off an even greater amount of territory. And, later on, if White ever pushed with the X-marked stone, Black's triangle-marked stone would automatically connect Black's surrounding string of stones.

B1 would also have left the White group with a classic problem, since no eyes have been made. To get them and some territory, White would have to choose one side or the other so Black could claim what was left! **The best kind of move is one that gains and threatens!**

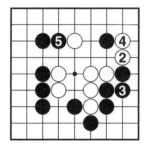

It is obvious that the solid move of B5 would wrap up the game. In the follow-up, a strong player would know that White couldn't be killed, but you are invited to try!

In any case, Black has more than 30 points, about twice as many as White.

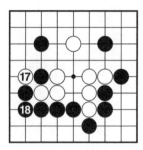

Instead, in the game, White has the opportunity to take the offense with the sente moves of W15-17. Now White is assured of two eyes besides having gained lots of territory.

But the game is not over!

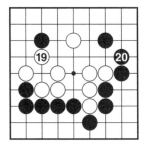 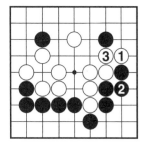

Because of the corner stone in the upper-left that Black threatens to connect with, White loses sente because B18 forces W19 to take in gote, since there are no further threats on the left side. So Black makes the smart move of B20.

B20 may look like gote but it isn't. Look at the difference if W1 had gotten there first. White would have had more points in the top three rows of intersections than all of Black's.

This kind of move is called *reverse-sente* and is counted at twice the value of a gote move. (If it had threatened Black at the same time, it would have been called *double-sente* and would have been worth twice what it is worth now.) These calculations will be discussed later.

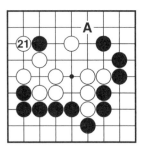

Next, White at least partially returns Black's errors on the left by playing the unnecessary W21. This should have been at A to expand territory after the damage done by B20.

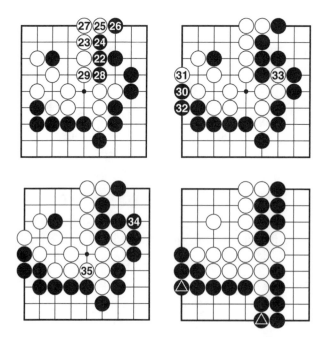

The end game quickly follows with no further surprises except that B22 should have been played at B24. In this battle of mistakes, Black wins a convincing victory. Despite what looks like a large White territory in the upper-left and narrow territory for Black along the two sides, Black has 31 points and White has only 16.

This game was won because of the special geometry of the Go board—all of Black's territory is on the edges so it took fewer stones to encircle it, while much of White's is in the center and needed additional stones to defend it.

Go Ranks

Igowin is like the old game of Tetris—if you win, your handicap goes down, if you lose, it goes up. When Igowin gave three stones, it indicated that the player had progressed from 25 kyu—the traditional starting point—to about 18-15 kyu.

Kyu ranks proceed up to 1 kyu and then you become a *dan*, and the ranks increase as you get better, as in other Eastern martial arts.

So Go can be looked at as a mental martial art, however, not everyone is "rank conscious" and Igowin's ranking shouldn't be taken too seriously, especially in the beginning. Players can win or lose a string of games quite by accident and quickly go up or down.

Nor are Igowin ranks necessarily indicative of what your rank is against players in the American or other Go associations, or on the Internet. One reason is that Igowin is a machine, and like all existing computer programs for the bigger boards, human players discover certain inherent weaknesses that can be exploited.

Official ranking in the Go organizations is acheived by winning or losing against other ranked players in tournaments and on the Internet. It becomes the average of the results of your individual games. The highest amateur ranks are now 9-dan, which is about the equivalent of a 1-dan professional and the highest professional rank is also 9-dan or, as it is sometimes written, 9-P.

In amateur ranks above 10-15 kyu, one kyu signals a difference of about one stone of handicap in 19x19 games, with the calibration being more precise once 9-kyu is reached. In 9x9 games, that figure can be divided by five.

Thus, a 4-kyu would play Black against a 1-dan with perhaps a smaller than ordinary komi, but would take 4 stones on a 19x19 board.

When two players who didn't know each other's strength have finished a game, each ten points difference in the score suggests that one handicap stone be added or subtracted for the next game. Once players have adjusted the handicap, if there are three victories or losses (or three out of four), the handicap is reduced or increased by one stone.

The amazing thing is that the benchmark for grading all the other ranks and determining the mark of amateur excellence—the 1-dan rank—equalizes itself worldwide, with a few adjustments for regional differences. For example, the Europeans, Koreans, Chinese, and the Internet servers set a higher mark than the Japanese or Americans do, so some of these might give an equivalently-numbered American dan a stone or two.

With professionals, however, the difference between a 1-dan and a 9-dan is only a few stones, because the competition is so intense and the advancement in grades so finely nuanced.

Styles and Advancing in Go

In the average Go career, generally there are rapid advances that begin to slow down after about 15 kyu. Also, please be aware that, as you progress, you will encounter plateaus that result from learning and concentrating on one aspect of the game while ignoring others.

Different players' styles are also a factor—some play better or worse against aggressive or cautious players. There are also *slow* and *fast* styles. These are not references to the speed of play—playing fast means quickly developing loose frameworks of stones while playing slow can mean that the player spends more time on developing tight groups that will become dangerous later on. But it can also mean making small moves when better ones are available, as the game in the next chapter will illustrate.

Some people think that go styles reflect the personalities of the players. However, the old adage that "The Go board is a mirror of the personality" shouldn't be taken too seriously. Nor should slack periods matter much, since your game will go through periods of development and integration in which you may be over-concentrating on the part of the game you are studying to the detriment of the rest. Also, plateaus are part of learning theory, and Go players are particularly aware of this since learning Go is like learning a language, but one in which there are winners and losers.

However, there are many who are unconcerned about their wins or loses or their rank, so they simply relax and enjoy playing beautiful games!

Exercises

There were many things about the handicap game that made it a good teaching game. We will combine these exercises with examples of basic things to think about as you play your own games.

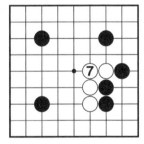

1. Always asking yourself, "Who has the weak groups?" is a good general principle to follow. How does it apply in a handicap game? What is the situation here? It is Black's move. Who is weak and who is not?

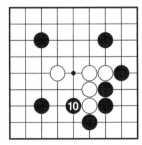 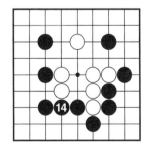

2. What do you think the Black player had in mind when trying to connect on the lower-left? And what wasn't on it?

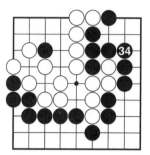

3. Why B34?

4. And, before that, what should have been played by Black?

Graduation Exercise

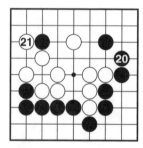

White's move is costly. Try to think of a proverb to remember so it doesn't happen to you!

Answers

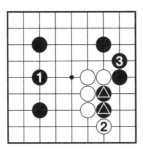 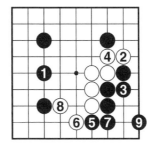

1. A sub-principle of this advice is that, because of the handicap, stronger players must often leave positions unguarded because they have no time to play the proper moves, but must quickly develop on other parts of the board.

Because the marked Black stones are not weak, Black can take over the left side with B1. As mentioned in the text, this is where White would have liked to go. Now White is left with crumbs. W2 in either place still leaves a string of stones. B5-7-9 is the prudent way for making good eye shape—against a strong player, any other way could cause trouble.

2. Two suggestions are:

A) "Try to avoid being split up" is a proverb, but in this case, it was applied to the wrong direction. Thinking about what is happening on the "big board" should always be the first consideration.

B) However, Black remembered that "Everyone makes mistakes," as the rest of the game demonstrated. It's how you try to take advantage of both your opponent's and your own that makes the difference between success and catastrophe.

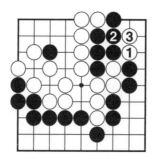

3. Enough said!

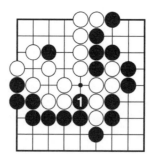

4. Atari!

Graduation Exercise

"Having a bad plan is better than having no plan at all," might be one. But it is still an indecisive move. Here's a story that will help you remember to ask yourself if you have a plan in mind before making a move.

In the *Zuo Zhuan*, an early-4th-century-BC chronicle, is one of the oldest references to Go playing in ancient Chinese literature. A minister is horrified when he finds out the treachery that a relative and friend have in mind.

> *Alas, Ning-tsze is dealing with his ruler not carefully, as he would at Go. How is it possible for him to escape disaster? If a Go player lifts his stone without definite object, he will not conquer his opponent. How much more must this be the case when one tries to take a king without a definite object? He is sure not to escape ruin. Alas that by one movement a family whose heads have been ministers for nine generations should be extinguished!*

So, before making your next move:

1. Beware being caught up in the heat of battles! That is one of the worst bad habits of even great players!

2. Don't think of handicap stones as encircling territory—think of them as "power points" that you can both build upon and sacrifice for future gains.

3. In many games, it is advantageous to force White to invade the corners—and hence be confined while your influence radiates outward.

CHAPTER SEVEN

Counting with Sente and Gote

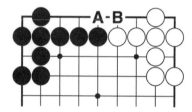

It is time to get serious about counting in the end game! if you know what you're doing, little points can add up to big points, and you can lose a lot if you don't. As a shortcut, you will save a lot of time if you know a few formulas.

For starters, what are end game moves like *A* and *B* worth?

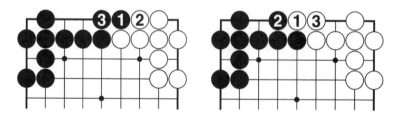

In this hypothetical situation, both groups have two eyes and are not in danger, so if Black gets to play first, White is left with two points and Black has four. If White plays first, the two groups have three points each. Moving first gains one point and makes the other lose a point for a total of two points for one side or the other. But is that the real value of the move?

The most important thing to remember is that, on the left, Black has to make two plays and White only one, so White is free to play elsewhere and pick up extra points.

On the right, the situation is reversed.

Thus, the first moves in these situations start with sente but end in gote.

Put simply, sente is when you "force" your opponent to answer you—but, it is up to the opponent and not you to decide this!

Let's look at another situation that is more complicated.

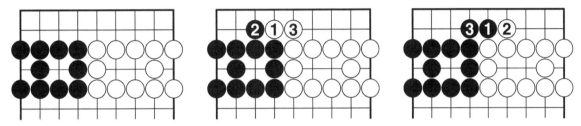

These stakes are higher along the edge. Again, both W1 and B1 start in sente but end with gote, so what is the true value of these moves?

As we saw before, one must consider the value of the next move by the other side, but there is also much more to think about.

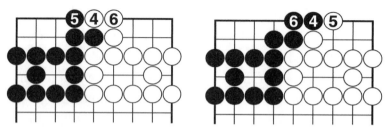

In the left diagram, White has nine and Black has eight.

On the right, White has eight and Black has nine. Getting in these last moves make a two point difference in the score.

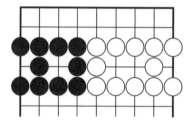

So, in a situation like this, and when there are many other situations on the board, how do Go players cope with the idea that not only does the value of the next move have to be calculated, but, if one has the ability, all the ones that follow as a consequence?

You can see that if a player makes a mistake and ends up in gote before working out what comes next, it could result in a long series of sente moves by the other side that would add up to a loss of many points.

This is how sente and gote are tied to counting and it is another lesson of how Go, at least as played by professionals, turns a game of efficiency into a scientific affair, especially in the early stages of games on bigger boards.

But since Go is so "big," even computers, let alone Go players, cannot "crunch" all these future moves, as they do in simpler games like chess and checkers. Computers might be able to do this someday in the distant future, but for now, humans are the champion Go players and all computer programs can be beaten by lowly amateurs. Why?

One reason is that humans are good at estimating these chains of values from patterns. Computers are not. This "feeling for form" is what turns Go into an art!

So what do Go players do?

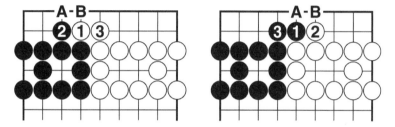

They assume that the chances of Black or White playing at A or B are about even because these moves are small if they don't affect the other strategic situations.

In the first example, Black has six and White has 12.

On the right, if Black moves first, both groups end up with nine.

The difference is three for each, making the first move "worth" six points, but it is in gote so Go players will say that the "actual" value is "about" three points.

This is because it is assumed that the move that follows will be close to that value, although, of course, this is not always so.

The exercises will elaborate on these considerations.

Exercises

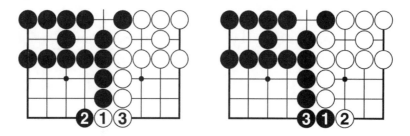

1. These seem to be typical gote end game moves, but the possibility of the other player moving first makes them something else. What is it?

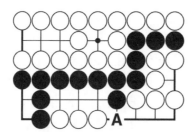

2. Is Black A a gote move or something bigger? What if White moved there?

Graduation Exercise

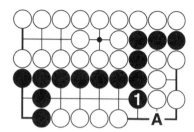

In this case, where the White group is smaller, is B1 sente? Is White's response at A gote or sente or something else?

Answers

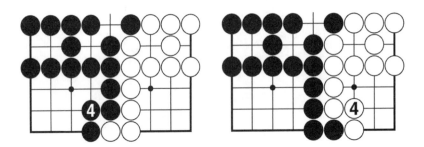

1. If W4, Black is left with 13 points and White has 11, and if B4 is played, Black has 15 and White has 9 for a seeming difference of four points. Both sequences end in sente, meaning that the values of the next moves must be added in.

Getting in these moves also prevents the other player from making a big invasion that would destroy the bottom territories. These invasions, however, would not threaten the life of the other group, so they wouldn't be played until the value of other moves reaches the sum of both of those territories plus the gains of each player. They would be valuable ko threats up to that point, so it would be foolish to play them too early, if there is a possible ko.

At that point, they would be considered double-sente moves in the sense that they would be sente and would be stopping a sente move, which would make them "twice" as valuable as an ordinary sente move.

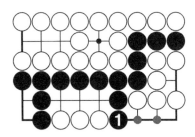

2. It prevents White from capturing 14 stones and the territory they sit on, plus five points of territory, and it gives Black eight points of territory plus three White stones for a total of 44. It is a gote move, however, because White does not have to answer—White can make a second eye on one of the marked places.

However, if White played there first, it would kill the Black group because White can make two eyes but Black would have only one. But killing Black would be a gote move for White because it would not affect any other position on the board. Thus, it is not a reverse-sente move, which would have made it worth "twice" what a gote move is worth.

In other words, for both sides, it is worth about half the size of the Black group and territory, plus the three White stones, since the value of the following moves have to counted.

It is "about" that size because Black would have a one-point sente move to the right of B1 that would threaten White's second eye. Thus, if White moved next to B1, it would be a one-point reverse-sente move, and would be played when the value of the moves had been reduced to one pointers, instead of half-pointers.

These calculations are only the tip of the iceberg of counting the value of moves in Go. As you get more acquainted with the game, you will discover that Go is not only "right-brained," intuitive and artistic, but it can also be a "left-brained" mathematician's paradise.

Graduation Exercise

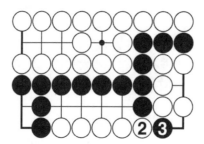

If White does nothing or tries W2, B3 will kill.

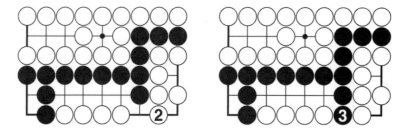

At first, the situation might seem to involve White's survival in gote—worth "half" the value of five stones and seven points of territory (since White gains one point by living).

But it is not gote if Black wants to make a second eye and save 14 stones, 10 territory points, and capture four White stones in gote, that is, minus the value of White's following move. At that stage of the game, especially if the follow-up move is small, players might call this *absolute sente*—a move that must be answered.

CHAPTER EIGHT
An Even Game

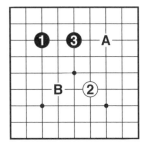

This game between two relatively weak amateurs has many good teaching points and is also a wonderful contrast of styles.

The commentary will not be too judgmental in the sense that strong players could easily make tricky moves based on long look-aheads and their deep knowledge of Go, but they would not mean much to beginners. Instead, the discussion will be principles-oriented and will try to explore some of the issues raised by players' choices of moves.

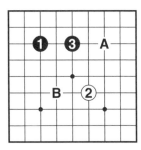

B3 may look over-concentrated to some players, who would prefer to extend to *A* or *B*, but it also could be said that Black is developing slowly but solidly.

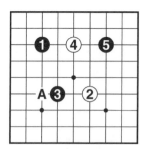

For example, with the faster, but not necessarily better, developing move of B3, if W4 *pressed down*, B5 could set up a second group. This would make a difficult game for White because Black would be using the sides and corners to fight in an outward direction while gaining territory within. White would then be stuck in the center with few prospects, especially because of komi.

So White would have to start a fighting game, perhaps with an attachment at A.

The Exercises will explore some of this line of play and will also include a discussion of some of the shapes used or suggested in this game.

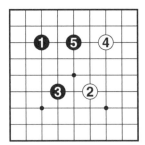 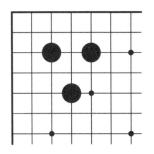 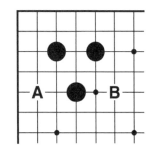

If White played in the vicinity of B5 in the last diagram, Black could then play at W3 and make a resilient shape called a horse's neck. A tighter shape, shown on the right, is called the dog's neck. It is very hard to cut across these two necks, and, if there is trouble, their shape is amiable for making eyes because of moves like A or B.

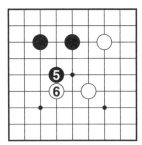

Keeping with this theme of tight development that is possibly preparing for future invasions of White's looser framework, with B5, Black prefers the tighter dog's neck to the looser horse's. Again, this may seem over-concentrated, but it is a style and is probably OK in this situation because White is stretched so thin on the right side—the two White stones can be easily separated. If that happens, it is usual that one side will escape and the other will die.

Another way of thinking is to go back to the concept of arms and legs extending from the stones. It is true that Black's stones are linked arm-in-arm, but their influence is limited to a relatively small part of the board. This gives White a lot of room to maneuver, so one could consider the amount of territory that is being staked out. After W6, it is easy to see who is doing more in that department.

But the business of staking out territory is often a vague concept because of its relation to future events. Again, there is a question of whether the distance between the marked White stones on the right is too far, so the idea of adding territory without re-enforcing a position of weakness is a debatable matter.

But there are even more considerations—some players who think they excel in fighting will often leave tempting gaps in their formations to invite the opponent to step into the ring.

In any case, this is a wonderful contrast in styles!

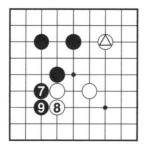

Black must block White's advance so W6 in the last diagram was played in sente.

W8 continues the assault and Black must meekly answer. Does this mean that playing sente moves is always a good idea? Looking at the whole board, is the marked White stone going to be able to work with White's industrious activities in the lower-center?

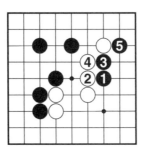 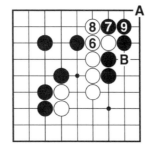

Among a number of possibilities on the right side, Black could invade with B1. White must connect with W6 and there are eyes around A and B. White would be left with nothing.

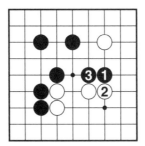 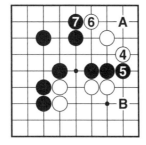

If White blocks the other way, one of the two separated groups is likely to die. Black A and B are both killing moves and White could only choose one to defend.

The details of the swan song of the lower group will be presented as an Exercise at the end of the chapter, though, if you have this position laid out on a board, you should try it now.

White has a way to correct the situation but is about to make a terrible mistake in direction.

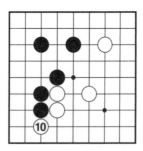 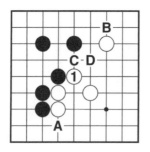 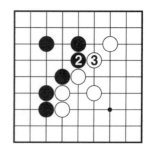

White keeps pushing and plays W10!

W1 would be best but then Black would have several choices. C is too passive, but *A-D* would offer hope. The bottom sequence is straightforward and the alternatives at the top are explored in a few pages, though it would have been much better to play them now.

If C (B2) is played, White would have a solid lead on the board, let alone with komi.

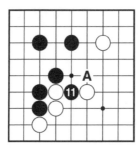 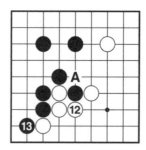

Again, the proverb says that "Having no plan is worse then having a bad plan." Unfortunately, B11 is both as both players ignore the vital area around A on the left.

Strangely, after the equally foolish B13, White will not take at *A* on the right, either.

By concentrating only on the local situation, they were not using whole-board thinking—undoubtedly the biggest problem for Go players of all strengths!

One tends to get caught up in the drama and automatically respond to the opponent's aggression, rather than taking a moment to step back and see what is on the whole board. For this reason, the Buddhists have a saying that progress in Go is a matter of lifting the "27 Veils of Ignorance" that keep us from seeing the true reality.

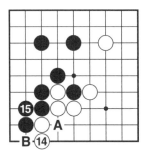

B15 is also absurd, and so was W14. If that corner area was important, White should have played W14 at A, because, when Black descends to A (which B15 could have done), White would have to play in gote to defend.

But that area is not important and these are end game moves. The big open area is in the upper-right, where the players should have been concentrating on.

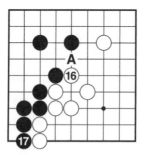

Finally, the center is captured by White! Possession of the center, especially on the smaller boards, can be quite important in controlling the flow of a game.

Meanwhile, Black keeps scratching for worms in the corner! The intuitive move would be A, but we have already shown that this leads to White's victory. Is there anything that Black could have done after White's big capture?

Invasions and Reductions

Invasions and reductions are an important part of the late-middle games of Go. Often their failures or successes are the key factors in defeats or victories.

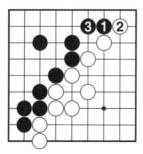

If Black could magically fill in the center, this would be a typical reducing maneuver. You should try out other results from this basic position to discover why drawing back is an important tool for securing areas like this, even if it ends in gote.

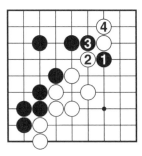

But the game situation is like this, so playing on the inside is an invasion of sorts, but the results are not good!

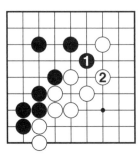 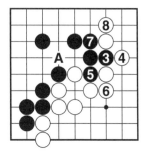

About the only alternative left would be B1, but that also ends short of the goal—and there is still the problem of A.

So, the game seems like it is over at this point.

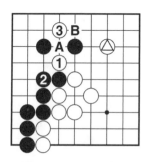
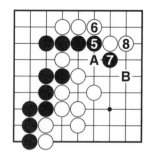

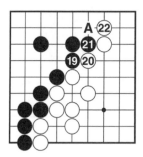

Apparently fearful of Black's meaningless moves, White meekly answers B17's threat at B by going worm digging too. What territory is left in contention on the bottom is absurdly small—and there are no follow-ups to match the huge areas at stake in the center around A.

To elaborate a little, the sequence on the right is what to do! Black connects at A, and White connects to the marked stone with B.

Black can keep pushing, but must defend at A, so White can *connect up* at B.

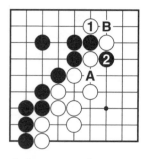

Black finally gets back on the track with B19 and the natural sequence follows to W22. Did you spot why White could not be greedy and play at A?

If White was careless (and even top professionals in top tournaments get careless once in a while!), B2 would be followed by White A and Black B.

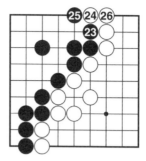

The game seems to be over, but is it really? Black seems to have 24 points and White seems to have 33 points and one prisoner. It appears to be a crushing victory for White.

Desperately, as should be done, Black looks around for a weak spot in White's armor!

A hint has been given as to where this might be, and it is a very common situation at the end of a game when one player has been greedy! Before you undertake the solution in the Graduation Exercise, give it some thought while you solve some problems suggested by earlier positions in this game.

Exercises

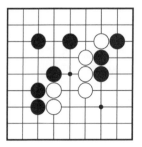 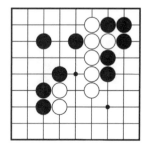

1. After the invasion, it is White's move. How can Black make two eyes?

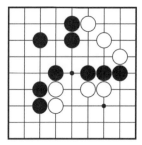

2. The game is over, and White has resigned, but the players linger on afterwards to see how Black is going to kill one group of White's choosing. It is White's move

The next few problems are some quirky situations from other games that would have readily revealed themselves by using the stone-counting method of scoring. However, even if you can't solve them at first, they will be easier to spot in your own games after you look at the answers. In other words, the idea is to "sense" them before the end of the game. They are all caused by greed and after you have looked at them, you will become like an all-knowing onlooker who would "never" try such shortcuts in your own games!

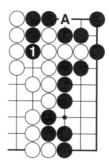

3. Trying to prevent White from making an eye, Black unwisely plays B1 instead of calmly making an eye at A. What is the likely outcome?

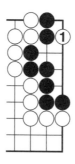 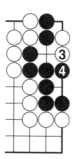

4. Black blithely ignores W1, thinking that if White plays W3, B4 is an adequate defense. But it isn't.

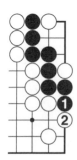

5. Don't be embarrassed if you don't see the solution of this right away. In a previous chapter there have been hints of what is to come. Recklessly pursuing every point in sente, B1 induces W2, which leaves Black with one less liberty.

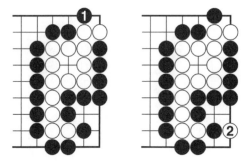

6. Black is trying to be clever and take away White's second eye with B1, but there are some details that were forgotten—such as good shape on the right side! Go players would call this *aji* ("Ah-ji"). In this case it is *bad aji* for Black and *good aji* for White.

We have already seen the clamp at work in the game against Igowin. In Japanese, this kind of clever move is called a *tesuji* ("te-su-jee). What is it good for here?

Graduation Exercise

Now, with your newly sharpened wits, we can return to the game that was featured in this chapter!

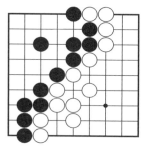

It is Black's move. If you are a beginning White player, you might have been impatient for the counting to begin! If you have some experience, though, and you are White, you might have some anxiety that Black might notice something. This is truly a graduating exercise!

Answers

You may not completely understand all the twists and turns of these problems, but try them out after playing a while. For now, the idea is to show the thinking process of Go players as they try one approach, then another, then another, until they think that something will work (or are sure it will not).

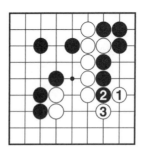 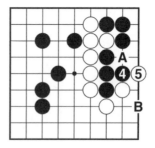

1. Here, the players struggle to take advantage of the peculiar geometry of the corners. After Black A answers the atari, and White B protects, Black does not have enough space for eyes.

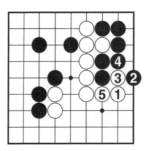 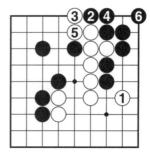

On the left is another failure sequence.

The secret is threatening to connect on the other side. To play it safe, Black can simply play B6 on the 1-1 spot, though it is possible to first play further out and pick up a few extra points. But "Safety First" is a good motto!

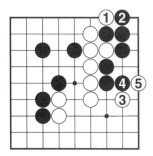 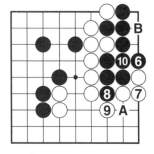

If White tries to forestall things, it still doesn't work.

Black can play at A or B to make two eyes. There are other possible ways for White to play after B2, but they don't work either. Try to find them!

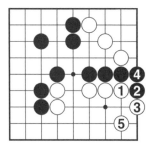

2. The lower-right area is larger so White defends it—generally, a move like W5 is better for making eye shape than a defensive move one line above it.

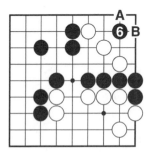 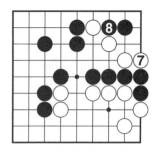

B6 is at the point of symmetry—always a good spot to aim for when defending or attacking! Even better, it can control the all-important eye-making points of A and B.

B8 is the important move—it should be clear that this case is closed!

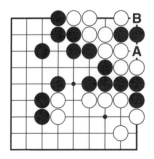 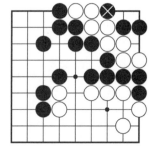

Except when there is a possibility of a seki! If the position on the right had resulted though negligence or good play (depending on whose side you are on), neither player would want to play at A—it would be self-atari.

As for B, it would be self-atari for Black to play there. If White played there and Black took with the X-marked stone to atari White, it would be a repeated position if White took back. White would have to find another move elsewhere on the board, and of course there are none. In effect, it's a ko!

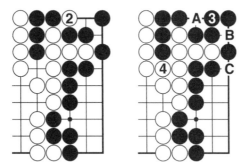

3. Black retakes after White A, but must fill in at B and C.

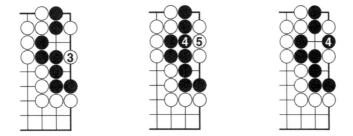

4. Black can either make a seki or try to win a ko in gote.

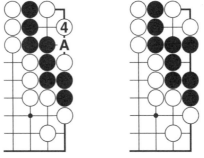

5. If B3 is elsewhere, W4 forces a seki since Black must take at A.

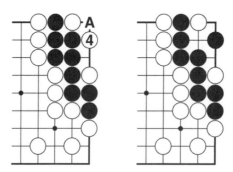

B3 creates a ko for life at A so the gote B3 on the right is correct. In Japan, this is called a *flower-viewing ko* because White has nothing to lose by playing it. Beware of apparently useless, but oddly placed stones, especially in the corners!

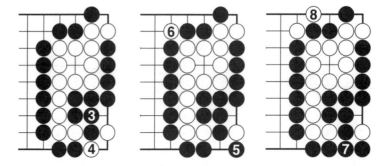

6. To prevent a thrown-in atari that resembles the crane's nest pattern of the Chapter One exercises, Black must play B3 which allows White to set up a ko.

Graduation Exercise

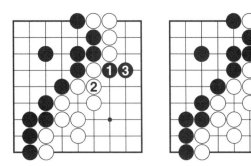

"'Where's there's smoke, there's fire!" applies equally well to the kitchen and the Go *ban* (which is a Japanese word for game board that you will see once in a while). Can Black survive?

W2 must protect and Black naturally descends. Note that by doing so, Black has gained two liberties and now has four. The White group above it has only three.

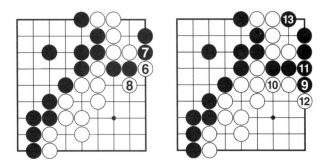

B5 was in the vital spot and death quickly follows.

CHAPTER NINE
A Big Ko

This rather astounding game was played by professionals. Breeze though it just to enjoy it, and then go back and test yourself by trying to spot the biggest threats and the whys and wherefores of its inner logic.

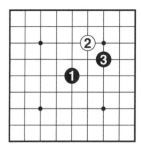 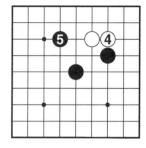

Since Black takes the center point, White must choose something not too far and not too close. B3 presses down with a knight's move.

B5 encircles White with a second knight's move. This is how to use knight's moves to attack, since there is plenty of room behind them to recover if they eventually get cut.

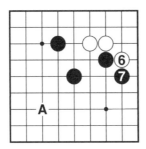 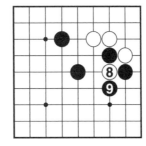

White wants to stabilize the group and is aiming to set up a second one around A. This would leave Black with very little.

Black doesn't like that idea, however.

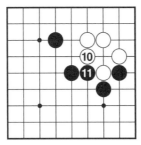 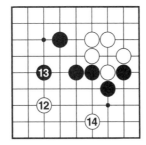

The possibility of a ko is set up, but at this point, it is not very important so White starts a group in the lower-left.

By using the bottom and lower-left sides as protection, White can safely make the long extension. This much more important than worrying about the fate of the upper-right, where, if pressed, White could make a small life with two eyes, but not much else.

Black, too, is busy setting up shop in the upper-left with a particularly good triangle shape formed with B13.

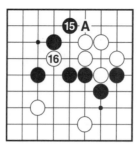 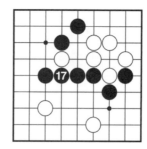

B15 initiates an attack on White.

Most beginners would block at A, but White has bigger plans. Black responds to White's *probe* at the center of the triangle shape by connecting with B17.

Probes are an important tool—with them, you can see which way the opponent thinks is important and act accordingly.

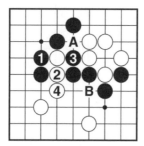

In this case, however, there is not much of a choice. If Black responded the other way, White A would put Black at a disadvantage, since it would be a scramble for life in the lower right. This would also leave the upper-right stones in a precarious position.

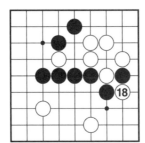
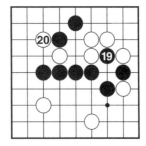

W18 makes the ko suddenly big and Black starts it. White makes the ko threat at W20 that threatens to take the entire top and leave Black with nothing.

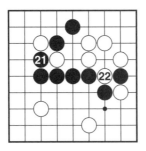
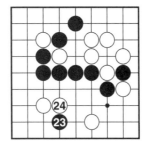

So Black responds and White takes back the ko.

B23 then threatens White's bottom group and White must respond with W24.

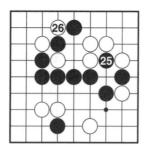

Black then gets to take back the ko with B25.

As you can see, these threats are much bigger than what the ko is worth, although if White eventually loses it, there would be a scramble for life and death in the upper-right corner, which White cannot yet afford to defend!

If White played in the upper-right, it would be in gote and Black would take the entire bottom-right. Then, while White defended the lower-left group, Black would take all of the upper-left.

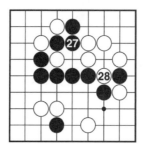 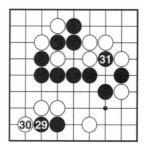

The struggle goes on! Perhaps you can see a smile or a gleam in the eyes of the players. This is when Go gets fun!

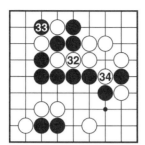
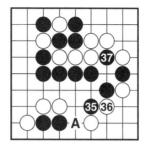

The values of the threats are getting smaller. Black would love to have a chance to play at A.

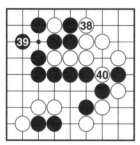
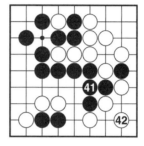

This is a long ko! Usually they go on for only a few moves, but this is extraordinary, particularly because the threats are relatively easy to understand. Note the nice eye-shape that W42 makes.

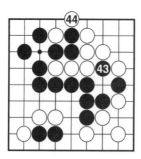 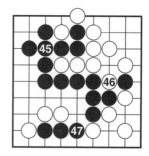

The ko is winding down to the last threats.

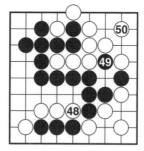

Soon, the question of who wins it will be irrelevant and this is how ko can be used as a strategic weapon to attain what one wants.

White could not afford to play W50 earlier in the game because it would have been a gote move to save the group—it wouldn't have threatened anything. Without the threats of the ko, Black would have then taken the bottom side. As it was, White kept Black on the defensive, forcing answers until at last White could maneuver to protect the upper-right group.

You will be able to see this process more clearly if you go back and look at it again. Once you do, you will have a better idea of how ko works and how to use it as it begins to crop up in your games.

Graduation Exercise

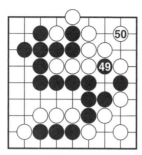

Can you show how the ko has become completely useless?

Answer

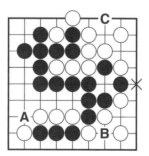

The first thing to notice is where the big ko threats are. Black has multiple threats at A and B, and at C if White was cut off from connecting at the X-marked spot. White, on the other hand, doesn't really have any.

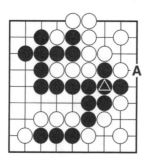

So let's suppose Black is magically able to fill the ko and get A in, which Black must play to prevent White from connecting on the side.

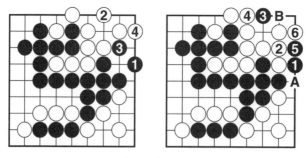

For teaching purposes, one creative way, though not the best in terms of points, is for White to grab the vital point with W2 and let Black take with B3, then get the second eye in the corner.

A more conventional method is to fill the ko. It doesn't make any difference if B3 tries to take what was the vital point—White can take with A and connect, or make two eyes with B. White is far ahead and Black must resign.

CHAPTER TEN

Elementary Handicap and Even Play on Large Boards

Some Modern Joseki and Fuseki

It's time to take what we've learned on the little boards and step up to the bigger boards. This chapter and the next are illustrated with full-size 19x19 boards, but the lessons will be fully applicable to the 13x13 size, which is what is recommended for your next games of Go.

However, as you will see, the principles of good play are easier to illustrate on the 19x19 size, so just scale things down a little for your 13x13 games and be aware that on the smaller board, control of the center is more important. You will see from the examples below how easy it is to cultivate that concept.

What follows is what every mid-kyu player knows something about, so the fact that star points are played on in this particular opening will point the way to playing and winning your handicap games against them as well as your even ones against players of your own strength.

The best way to use these last two chapters is to lay down these openings with the aid of the book and then play out some games by yourself or with friends. Some of of the ideas of what to do next will also be suggested in Chapter 11.

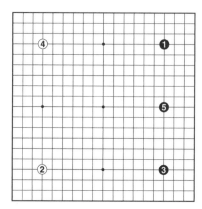

This is called the *three-star point opening* or the *san ren sai* ("San-ren-sigh") in Japanese. It was invented there in the 1930s as a response to the more territorial games that had been played for more than 300 years. Since then, it has been improved and modified by Japanese, Chinese and, most lately, Korean professionals. Much of what follows is some of their latest thinking, as discussed with much greater detail in *A Dictionary of Modern Fuseki: The Korean Style* (Kiseido 2004).

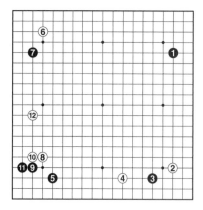

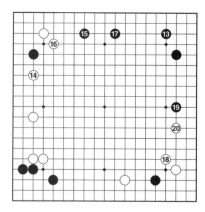

Contrast the san ren sai opening with a game played in 1670 above (notice Black's ideal *double wing formation* in the upper right), and one below played in 1926 (which has been called one of the most spectacular games ever played).

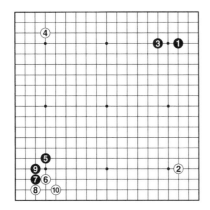
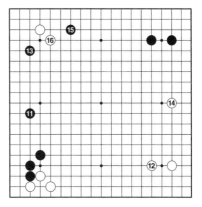

These were "old-style" games that emphasized control of the corners instead of immediate, one-move outward influence.

The early stages of a Go game are called the *fuseki* ("fu-se-kee") in Japanese, so the san ren sai was called the New Fuseki. Note that it is a parallel fuseki, while the two earlier games were diagonal fusekis. Both patterns remain equally effective.

Within the fusekis are sequences of plays that have been proven to yield equal local results for both sides in terms of territory and influence. These are called *joseki* ("joe-se-kee") and new ones developed and old ones were discarded for hundreds of years.

Most players and teachers do not advise that joseki be memorized. Instead it is better to use common sense and try to apply reasonable playing principles to the situation.

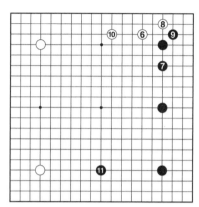

Here, White approaches and Black extends with a one-space jump. Both sides are satisfied after they establish corner positions and extend further along the sides.

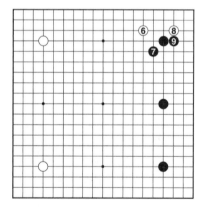
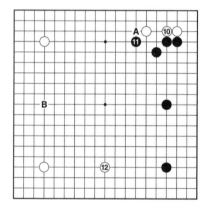

Black can also play a diagonal move of B7 and this is a typical result. White has corner territory and has dampened the influence of Black's large framework.

Depending on what happens and the styles or inclinations of the players, *A* and *B* are probably going to be big points to watch in this game—*A* because of the territory involved and *B* because the side-star points are always good for breaking up *moyo* ("moy-yo") frameworks.

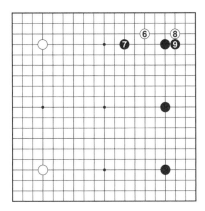 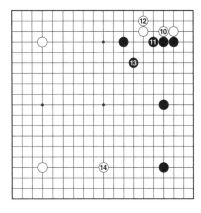

Somewhat similar is the result when Black is fearless and pincers W6. This is one good way to respond.

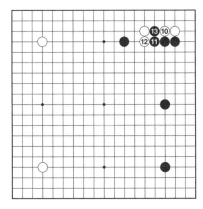 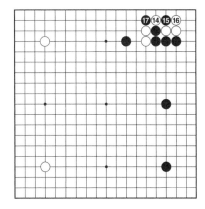

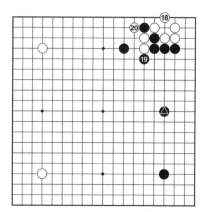

This is another valid way. In both cases, Black wants to keep the framework by using the marked stone as an anchor. However, as you progress, you will find that it is usually not a good idea to use frameworks to simply amass territory—they often must end with gote moves so the other player will profit more. (Remember, subtract the value of the next move from the points gained by a gote move). Instead of gote, use the threat of the moyo's power to cause trouble in sente!

Let's pause here for a moment and look back at the first diagram to consider the choices that White and Black had to make in these sequences.

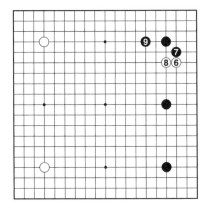
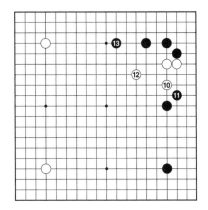

For example, if the invasion was on the wrong side, the White group would have no eyes, no territory and would be under attack. While Black would not get all of the upper- and lower-right sides, White would certainly be at a huge disadvantage.

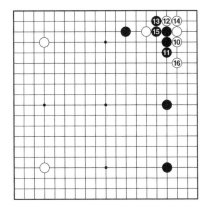

Black has clearly made the wrong choice of direction to block White. Not only is the framework destroyed because White can continue on down the right side, but the pincer stone is too close to Black's wall to be effective or efficient. Always try to achieve the largest extension when blocking!

Exercises

You probably won't be able to come up with right answers (at least not right away), but try to lay out these positions and experiment before looking them up. That's how you will become familiar with them and learn something about how to handle White in handicap games.

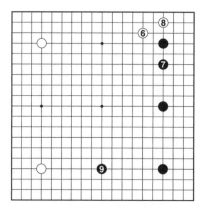

1. B9 plays for influence. What will White do and how should Black respond?

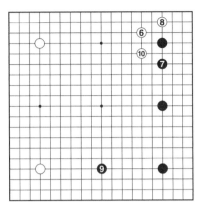

2. In contrast to the answer of Exercise 1, White surprises Black by jumping up with W10. How would you play?

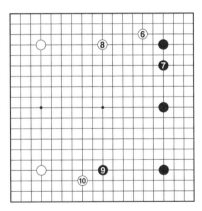

3. After this sequence, what is a natural move for Black on the bottom?

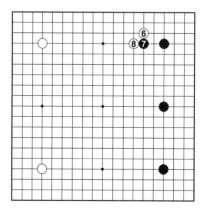

4. Professionals are touchy about letting White settle solidly along the side, but you will see this pattern in amateur handicap games. What do you think is the next logical play?

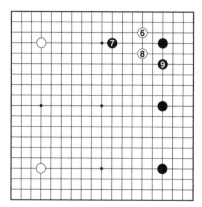

5. The two-space pincer is also useful to know about. By now, you may be getting ideas about what should come next and what each side would want to do after that.

Graduation Exercise

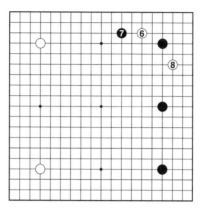

Even strong players sometimes quiver when White makes the *double approach*. As you will discover, there are many responses, but what is the simplest way?

Answers

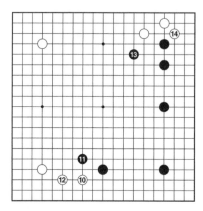

1. Look at the broad implications—again White has territory and Black has influence—both their stones are working well with each other!

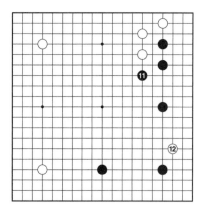

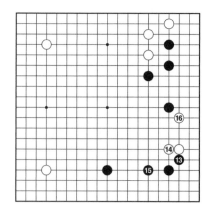

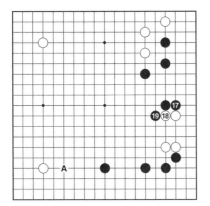
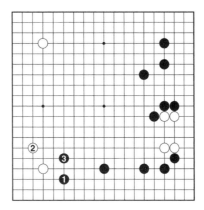

2. White often plays like this in a handicap game. Black should try to contain White on the right side and expand towards A with later moves like B1-B3.

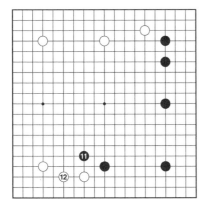
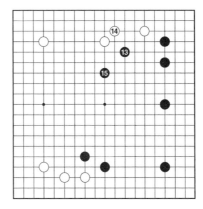

3. B11 and B13 preserve the moyo and force White to respond. The game is even at this point.

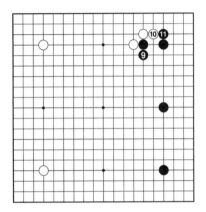 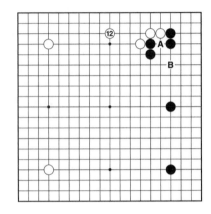

4. This attach-and-extend joseki is popular, although playing B to prevent the cut at A should probably be used only until you realize how, by letting the cut happen and just moving along with White, Black can make tremendous fourth-line profit!

Second-line profit has been called the "line of defeat." Third-line is OK, but fourth and fifth are the best.

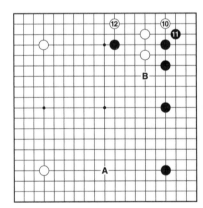

5. After this, but not necessarily right away, Black would like to play at both A and B, but so would White! You should try out both ways.

Graduation Exercise

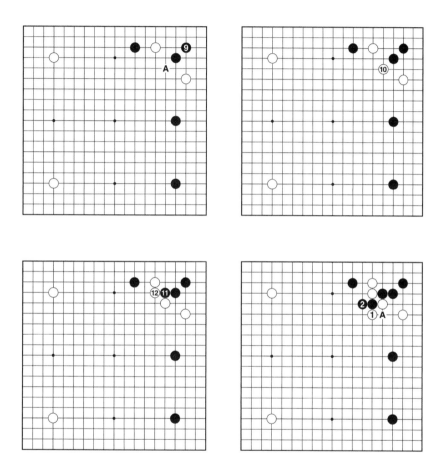

Because getting boxed into the corner is generally an unpleasant experience, Black A—"running away to get stronger"—would be better against a wider double approach, or if there was no friendly pincer stone close by to work with. This was demonstrated in the two "old-style"

games and it is also true for handicap Go, whether or not there are stones on the side-star points.

W10 is natural, but the pincer stone starts to exert its power because a cut is inevitable.

It might be tempting for White to atari at W1, but then A must be played and this would lose the initiative. Ataris are not always the best play.

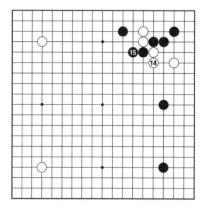

B15 completes the sequence.

In the last part of the next chapter, we will see how some of the fuseki principles of this chapter can be developed into the free-flowing atmosphere of another professional game.

CHAPTER ELEVEN

Strategies on Bigger Boards

Extending: A Review of Fundamentals

Players often talk of tactics and strategies as if they were different sides of the game, but actually they are opposite sides on the same coin. Take, for example, the concept of extending, which we saw taking place in the last chapter.

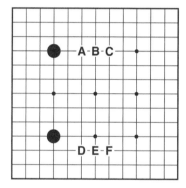

In an attempt to gain influence and territory, Black can extend to all these points between *A* and *F* with varying degrees of safety and danger, as you have seen on the 9x9 boards and perhaps intuited in the last chapter.

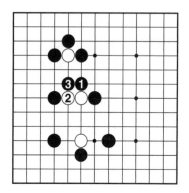
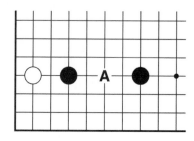

For example, an intruding White stone poses little difficulty for Black with the *one-point jump*, a little more with the *two-point*, and a considerable amount with the *three-point jump*, where the possibilities for making trouble have multiplied exponentially.

This is particulary so if there are other White stones in the area. Black is vulnerable at A.

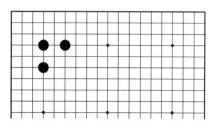
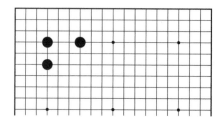

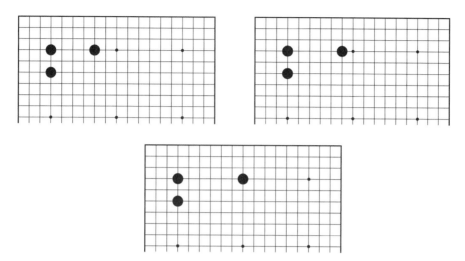

But things get much more interesting, as we saw, when extensions from these extensions are taken into consideration—in other words, when the whole board is taken into consideration.

Which of these five extensions feels more comfortable to you? The one-point extensions seem over-concentrated, the two- and three- less so, the four-point follows the proverb, "Extend one more intersection than the wall you are working from." The last might seem a bit too much, but that will depend on what is going on the right side and, as you will see, what the player's strategy and style is.

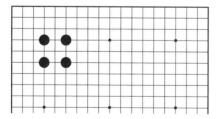

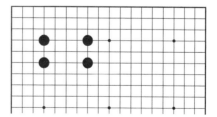

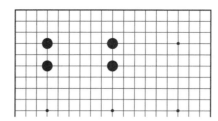

From this comes the idea of forming boxes to accumulate territory and influence. This is a good principle to follow, especially in handicap Go. Why?

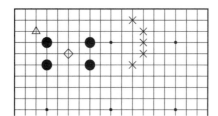 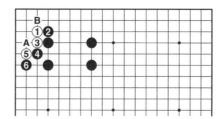

Black's weak point in the diamond-marked area is pretty well covered and, forgetting about the left side for a moment and just looking at the right, you can see how far the influence extends! This is quite a powerful formation. But what about the underbelly, marked by the triangle?

The prospects for White are not good. If Black plays in the right direction and lets the stones work together, White is left with two weak spots at A and B.

If B2 at W3, White will live but Black will have greater outward influence. Try this out.

What would happen in real play is that White would usually approach from the outside and use the threat of making a live group in the corner to gain some leverage. But that is a subject for advanced study!

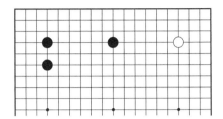
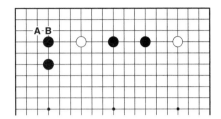

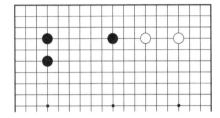

Let's get back to basics. Go is a game with two players, so what are the possible outcomes if there is a White stone in the other corner?

Extending on the idea of extensions, though it may not be played right away, Black can extend while White can invade at Black's vulnerable point. Of course, all this will depend on what is happening on the rest of the board. In any case, the corner questions hovering around A and B are suddenly brought into play.

On the other hand, White can extend and pass the question of playing elsewhere or defending back to Black. However, these points are useless to discuss any further without taking into consideration the other stones on the board, as the following professional game will vividly demonstrate.

A Top Professional Tournament Game

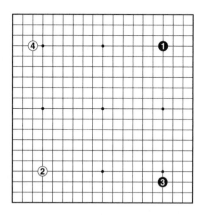 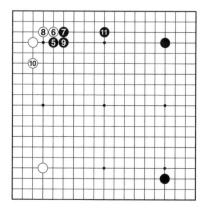

This was the beginning of Game 2 of the 1991 *Kisei*, Japan's annual highest-ranking tournament. At that time, it was the second-richest tournament in the world, worth about $320,000 to the winner. In this best of seven series, after six games, the final was decided by an agonizing half-point!

Following the geometry of the Go board, Black and White staked out the corners and cautiously *approached* each other. The exchange in the upper-left is called a 3-4 joseki since that is the point where it starts.

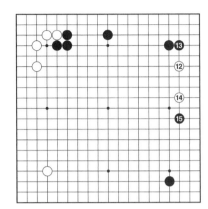 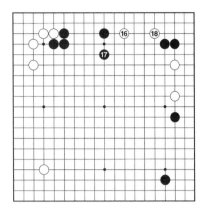

In the upper-right, Black responded to White's low approach by a solid, territorial move. Black was not going to be budged out of the corner! In fact, the style of the player was called "Subway Go" by a player who called his own style "Cosmic Go" because he habitually played for control of the center with large frameworks, like those in the last chapter.

Looking at Black's corner power, White naturally extended to make the beginnings of a stable group. He didn't want to be caught by a pincer!

To keep the balance of territory even, W16 invaded, so Black and White traded responses with equal gains for both.

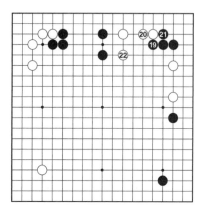
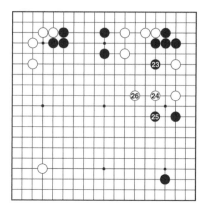

White climbed out into the center and Black stabilized the corner. At this point, it was any-one's game!

A similar process occurred on the right side. What was really going on, however, was that both players were looking at the wide-open spaces on the bottom and left. Each would have liked to end the side skirmishes in sente to move into these areas first.

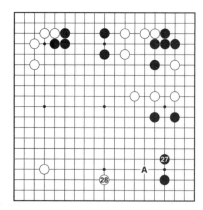
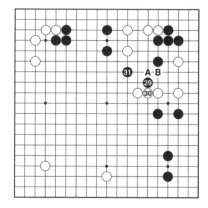

It was commented that B27 could have been at A, making a bigger but looser framework. In any case, after this, W28 was the first move on the wide-open bottom and the game began to get very complicated.

Black wanted to get out and surround White, so the *peep* of B29 was made, forcing W30. Peeps can be very useful tools, but one should use them with caution, since it also meant that Black's knight move was vulnerable at A or B, a defect that B31 had to repair. The result, however, was a strong and resilient shape.

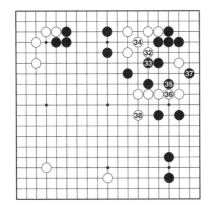 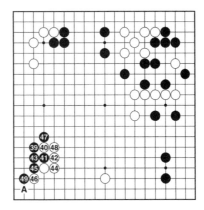

After more intricate and well thought-out maneuvering in the upper-right (W34 was called "one of the great moves of Go history" for example), Black got to play first in the lower left. The result was a solid corner group with influence radiating up the side to fend off White's power in the upper-left. After B49, White played A and we invite you to see what the consequences might have been. Eventually, White won by 4½ points after the komi of 5½ points was taken into consideration.

We hope this encourages you to play out more professional games and try their moves in your own!

Your Games

This chapter ends with an eye toward the future. Another handy way to see what playing on bigger boards is all about is to take some opening positions and continue your games from there. We suggest that you use a 13x13 board and simply reduce the lessons of the latter part of this chapter by an intersection or two. for example, try playing out these positions by yourself or with a friend to see what happens.

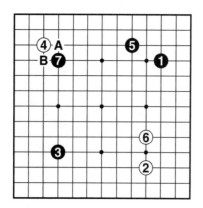
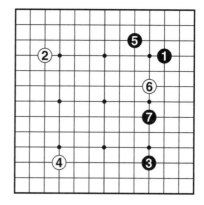

The *shoulder hit* of B7 forces a decision, but neither choice is welcomed by White, who will be confined to the corner in gote, while Black's double-wing-like power exudes all over the board, especially after the center is taken!

On the right, play this out because W6 seems to be a mistake. B7 not only pincers White, but makes a nice extension up from the lower-right corner. White will now have a weak group running towards the center, so Black can pursue and make territory and influence on the sides. One of the reasons for playing out professional games is that you will learn how to handle this kind of situation. The next chapter will tell you how to get some of these games in books and on the Internet.

CHAPTER TWELVE

Where to Go for More Go

If you feel you need more preparation before going on to bigger boards, *Go Basics*, my second book from Tuttle, features an intense game-oriented workout on 9x9 boards. The first, *Go! More Than a Game*, has two 13x13 and one 19x19 games that will give you enough Go knowledge to make you conversant with any Go player. It is also the only book with an extensive history of the game and its involvement with Eastern and Western culture, science, and history.

Online, out of the more than 1000 worldwide websites devoted to Go, the American Go Association's site, www.usgo.org, is perhaps the one to look at first. The Resources section is particularly valuable because it lists where you can find anything in the world of Go, including clubs, web servers, players and teachers of all strengths and nationalities. You can also subscribe to the AGA's twice-weekly free e-journal that will keep you posted on everything that is "Go-ing" on.

As for books, Yutopian, Slate and Shell, Samarkand, and Hinoki all publish fine books, but the only series for advancing up to the mid-kyu level and beyond are Kiseido's Graded Go Problems, Elementary Go, and Mastering the Basics collections. Kiseido's quarterly *Go World*, has excellent commentaries on current professional games, tournaments and players, as well as problems and instruction on all levels. Also, its website houses a fine collection of Japanese *ukiyo-e* woodblock prints that colorfully portray life and Go playing as they once were during the Edo period.

Glossary

aji: A condition in a position or group of stones that offers potential for play; aji may be good or bad.

atari: A condition that occurs when a move occupies the second-to-last liberty of an opponent's stone or group, thus threatening to capture it.

Baduk (or Paduk): The Korean word for Go.

dan: The highest set of rankings in Japanese and Western Go. Amateur rankings go from 1 dan to 7 or 8 dan, depending on the country. Professional ranks go from 1 to 9 dan. Commonly used terms are: *Shodon*: a 1 dan; *Nidan*: a 2 dan; and *Sandan*: a 3 dan.

fuseki: The opening stage of the game.

gote: To play last in a local encounter; the opposite of sente. Gote loses the initiative.

Igo: The Japanese word for Go.

joseki: A formalized sequence of moves that gives an even result. They are usually restricted to the corner.

ko: A board position that requires a player to make a move elsewhere before recapturing after the opponent has just captured a stone, to avoid re-creating a former board position(called the super-ko rule); one of the key strategic elements of the game. *flower-viewing ko:* A ko where there is little potential loss for the initiator but could be costly for the opponent.

ko threat: A move that is worth more than a ko that the opponent must answer so a player can retake the ko.

komi: The advantage for going first is compensated by komi. The standard komi in Japan has been increased to 6½ points to correspond with Korean and Chinese standards.

kyu: The lower rankings in Japanese and Western Go. Kyu ranks ascend from 25 kyu to 1 kyu.

moyo: A large territorial framework.

Nihon Ki-in: The chief Japanese Go Association, located in Tokyo.

rules: The rules of Go can be made exceedingly simple or excruciatingly complicated. There are at least a half dozen rule sets that are used around the world, but they differ only in minor ways. It is beyond the scope of this book to offer more than a cursory review.

Most Westerners use Japanese rules in which prisoners are counted and dame stones at the end of the game are irrelevant to the score. In the Chinese method of counting, no prisoners are taken. They are returned to their bowls. When no more plays are possible, all trapped stones are taken off the board and the remaining area and stones of one player are counted. If the total is more than 180½ (half of the 361 points of the Go board) plus or minus komi, then that player wins. Komi is half what it would be by the Japanese method. There are minor differences from Japanese rules in that stones inside a seki are counted and there is an advantage in playing last. Both rule sets prohibit suicide moves. Ko is also treated differently under various systems, but the main idea is that no board position can repeat itself (the "Super-ko rule"). One other point is that Black must give one point for each handicap stone.

seki: A position in which neither side can capture the other. The points in a seki are not counted, but in Chinese rules, the stones are.

sente: To have the ability to choose where to play next; to have the initiative. It is the opposite of gote. *Absolute sente:* A move that must be answered or the game is lost. *Double sente:* Worth twice as much as a sente move. It is a sente move that also prevents a sente move of the opponent. *Reverse sente:* A move that prevents a sente move of the opponent. It is approximately equal to a sente move in value.

tesuji: A clever move.

Wei Ch'i (or Wei Qi): The Chinese word for Go.

Three Boards To Play On

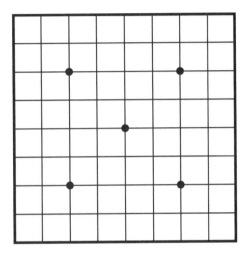

This board and the 13x13 and 19x19 boards that follow are meant to be copied and enlarged. Playing pieces can be easily made from pennies and dimes, small poker chips, or, perhaps like the first games of Go, colored beans or pebbles.

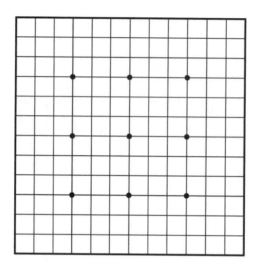

A 13x13 board.

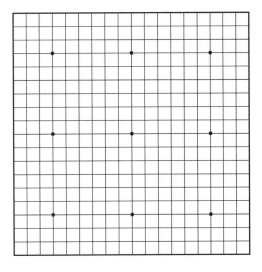

A 19x19 board.

About the Authors

Peter Shotwell is an internationally known expert on the relationship of Go to Eastern and Western philosophy, literature, and history. He has been writing about Go for over twenty years and has lived in China, Tibet, and Japan while researching the origins and background of the game. He is also the author of *Go! More Than a Game* and *Go Basics*.

Susan Long is a learning specialist who has held prestigious faculty positions in Boston and New York City private schools and universities. For many years, she has used Go in curriculum development and to work with students of all ages.